Alpana Pours

ALPANA SINGH

Alpana Pours

ABOUT BEING A WOMAN, LOVING WINE *and* HAVING GREAT RELATIONSHIPS

With Robert Scarola

Illustrations by Julia Anderson-Miller

ACADEMY
CHICAGO

Printed in 2006 by
Academy Chicago Publishers
363 West Erie Street
Chicago, Illinois 60610

Cover photograph by Erica Dufour
Cover and interior design by Sarah Olson

© 2006 by Scarola & Singh, LLC

Printed in the U.S.A.

Library of Congress Cataloging-in-Publication Data
on file with the publisher

ISBN-10: 0-89733-546-5
ISBN-13: 978-0-89733-546-1

For the first time since the Gallup Poll began keeping track in 1992, more Americans say their alcoholic beverage of choice is wine, not beer.

—*Chicago Tribune*, July 26, 2005

52% of those surveyed want to know more about wine.

—*Zagat Survey*

For Charles and Jackie

Contents

Introduction

SUCCESS WITH WINE, SUCCESS IN LIFE

Wine . . . is Everywhere!

A lot of us start by drinking Boone's Farm at school, or maybe we start drinking wine because we get a kick out of names like Fat Bastard, Two-Buck Chuck or Goats do Roam (a fun Cotes du Rhone style wine from South Africa). Let's face it, country farms and oddball names are less intimidating than something originating from, say, Bordeaux or Hermitage. And we live in a society where wine, although popular, is often over-intellec-tualized and shrouded in pretension to the point of becoming downright scary.

The good news is that it's really easy to get comfortable with wine because there are over 45,000 varieties in this great big world to choose from. As of Spring 2005, it is a fact that every state in the U.S. produces at least one wine.

Wine is everywhere . . . it is *the* universal adult beverage. Given all the choice, having fun with, and understanding, wine can result in great personal satisfaction and professional and social advantage.

The Alpana Files

Since I host *Check, Please!*, a restaurant review show on Chicago public television, people often ask me about wine and good places to eat. They also ask me about me. Over the last few years I have jotted down what I call "The Alpana Files," a journal filled with stories, lists and bits of advice to help me answer questions as far ranging as, "How was your first taste of wine?" to "How do you open a bottle of champagne?" For your wine and lifestyle benefit, I've sprinkled these nuggets throughout this book. I hope you find them fun and informative.

Now, Why Bother Listening to Me?

For five years I was the Master Sommelier at Everest, dubbed by one local dining critic "the most romantic restaurant in Chicago." Being around all that romance provided me with a monster database about how couples interact publicly during every stage of every kind of relationship. By spending a few moments at a table talking with guests about what wines they might enjoy, I became pretty good at sizing up the general shape of a couple's relationship. I could tell if they were in new love, unrequited love, unfaithful love, long-term love, conciliatory love, creepy love, platonic love, love in its final stages or love gone wrong.

All this exposure to couples "in love" and what wines they ordered gave me the insight I needed to tell what wine my restaurant guests might enjoy. It also helped me with my own relationships and taught me how wine can be part of making social interaction a whole lot nicer and easier.

What Wine Shouldn't Be

Working at restaurants, I saw firsthand all the anguish people can go through just to order a bottle of wine. Wine should never, ever be a point of frustration, shame, intimidation, confusion or conflict. Wine should be something that you have fun with and share with others; a joyful experience leading to a little bit of inebriation and hopefully to high-quality canoodling and then some.

From the Alpana Files: Sideways was a Good Thing

After the film *Sideways* came out, I noticed many more men and women ordering Pinot Noir. This was good: the movie helped expand people's knowledge and appreciation of wine. And yes, there was a slight decrease in the sale of, to quote Miles, the film's amateur wine expert, "f—king Merlot."

Wine is a Freeing Adventure

Since I'm an Indian-American, 29-year-old, female Master Sommelier, people often ask me how I got into wine. Well, obviously no one can honestly say, "When I was a child, I often lay awake dreaming about becoming a Master Sommelier." When I was younger, I had many varied interests in the arts and sciences and I was pretty confused about what I wanted to be when I grew up. Fortunately, wine became my key to finding my professional niche without having to give up the things I enjoy.

With wine as my profession, I get to visit some of the most interesting and beautiful places in the world—and I love to travel. Going to these wonderful wine places also allows me to fulfill my life-long passions for art and cultural diversity.

Since wine is a living thing, I can pursue my interests in organic chemistry, the environment and natural science. While I do have an inner geek that likes science and math, I am also a crazy romantic. With every bottle I try, alone or with others, I open myself up to wine's unique history, adventures in new flavors from interesting places, sensory excitement—in short, the romance of wine.

Wine Can Be Freeing for Anyone

If you're an interior designer, you can enjoy wine because there is an amazing amount of wine-related artwork and architecture. If you are a geologist, you can enjoy wine because of its connection to the soil. If you're a math major, you can enjoy the precise science and numbers involved in wine making. If you're a lawyer or civil servant, you can enjoy wine because of its connection to history and government. You name a profession and I bet I can find a way to relate it to wine.

Wine can free you to do things you like to do . . . and if I somehow forgot to mention this earlier, it tastes damn good too!

Wine and Gender Stereotypes

As much as I hate to say it, there seem to be certain gender-based wine stereotypes. The stereotype is, women like white and men like red. I'll go into this sexual dynamic in greater detail in the next chapter, but now I'll touch on this as a foundation for other notions we're about to cover.

Rather be Dead than Drink Red

Some women may find that red wine is heavy or has a bitter taste, or tannins give them a headache. I can't tell you how many times I've heard women announce, "I don't like any red wines!" To help them get beyond common misconceptions about red wine, I always recommend that these women try lighter red wines with fewer tannins, like Pinot Noir, Sangiovese, Zinfandel, Gamay or even Rosés.

White Flight

Men who think white wines are an effeminate drink will refuse to try Chardonnay or Pinot Grigio because that's what "the little woman" likes. To help the boys get over this prejudice, I recommend they try a full-bodied Gewürztraminer. We in the wine biz often joke that this Alsatian powerhouse, with its powerful aromatics, is a white wine trying to be a red.

From the Alpana Files:
Me & Wine...the Early Years

I Got into Wine on a Dare

While I was in junior college in Monterey, California, I wanted to work as a server at Montrio, a high-end restaurant. During the interview I was asked if I knew anything about wine. In late adolescent honest-speak, I replied, "They're made from grapes, right?" When she heard that, the manager said she would put my name on a hostess waiting list. Well, I realized that if I wanted to be a server there—and I did—I would have to learn a reasonable amount about wine. So I went out, bought a copy of *Wine for Dummies*, and proceeded to cram all weekend long. I went back on Monday, and offered chapter and verse about wine to the astonished restaurant manager. She was so impressed, she gave me the job. This kid was kind of in the wine business! I became fascinated by wine and started to read anything I could lay my hands on about the nectar of the grape. My fixation did not go unnoticed; suddenly I attracted the attention of a real-life sommelier who quickly became my mentor in all things wine.

My Wine Epiphany

Not long after being hired at Montrio, I was standing at the bar waiting for my drink order when my boss walked over and handed me a glass of red wine. I asked, "What is it?" He replied, "Shut up and taste it." On rolling some around in my mouth, I suddenly saw rainbows. The stuff absolutely blew me away. I could taste every aspect of the Charles Melton from Australia. It was totally clear for me. There was wonderful, comforting nutmeg and deep rich plum in this soft red wine. I got it, and it made me feel good. It gave me pleasure and I wanted that pleasure, like having a really great gooey fudge brownie over and over again. Years later I met Charles Melton. It was like having a religious experience. I told him, "Mr. Melton, you are the reason I'm in the wine business."

That sip of Charles Melton was the moment when wine became more important to me than anything, even a steady boyfriend or a passing grade. That very night, I told my mentor that I wanted to go totally *wine pro*. His first reaction was to ask me if I wanted to study agriculture for years and learn about making wine or join the fun side of the biz and sell wine for a living. Hmm? I wondered? Gee? Now? Okay . . . I'll take fun! He then said that if I studied very hard, I could eventually pass the Court of Master Sommeliers exam. He promised to make a call to get me a day job at Nielsen Brothers, a Carmel-by-the-Sea food/wine shop, saying, "Alpana, you need to surround yourself with wine. Nielsen's is a good place to start." Since I was on a mission, I didn't wait for him to call. The very next morning, I went to the shop and told the manager, "I'm nineteen and I want to be a Master Sommelier. I'll dust off bottles, whatever it takes. I'll work for free." The friendly store manager said he'd think it over and asked me to come back the next day. As you can imagine, I spent a sleepless night. When I went back to the shop, he said, "Can't have you work for free, Alpana. Let's say ten dollars an hour?"

Breaking the Wine News to Mom

Spending days at Nielsen's and nights at Montrio, absorbing anything I could about wine, I secretly cancelled all my classes. Like all mothers, mine can sense a disturbance-in-the-force when it comes to her headstrong daughter. I knew she knew something had drastically changed and that I wasn't going to be able to keep it under wraps. Before I headed off to work one morning, there was a scene between Mom and me reminiscent of a bad '80s situation comedy, as I broke the news about my new and very atypical Indian vocational choice. To understand this, you need to know that all Asian-Indian parents are determined that their children will become doctors.

Announcer: And now, its time for *Bolly-Mom & Me*, the funny and highly sentimental, day-to-day story of a hardworking immigrant Mom and her lovely, talented and ambitious late-teenage daughter. Tonight's episode: "Breaking the Wine News to Mom."

Alpana: Uh, Mom, did I tell you I took a job at Nielsen Brothers?

Mom: What are you doing there? You have a job. What about school?

Alpana: I'm working in the wine department of the store.

Mom: What about Montrio, the restaurant? Aren't you still working there?

Alpana: Oh, I work at Nielsen's during the day and Montrio at night.

Mom: And what about going to school?

Alpana: Well, ah, uh, I dropped all my classes. I'm not going back to college, Mom.

Mom: What do you mean!?

Note how Moms squeeze it out of you with shorter and shorter questions.

Alpana: Well, Mom, I want to be a Master Sommelier.

Mom: Sommelier? What part of the body does the sommelier work on? How do you plan to pay for medical school? You need two jobs to do this? That's years and years of work ahead of you. Are you able to manage that?

Alpana: It's not being a doctor, Mom. It's about wine. I want to become a wine expert. Someone who knows all about wine.

Mom: Wine!? Wine. What are you going to do with wine!? You drink wine now? When did that start? That restaurant, I'm going to call them about you drinking wine.

Alpana: Mom!

Mom: How am I going to tell my friends that my daughter is in the wine business!? I do not understand this sommelier! What are my friends going to say? My daughter is in the wine business now!? This is really something. I do not know, Gigi, this does not sound good.

Gigi is my nickname.

Alpana: Gotta go, Mom! Call you from work!

(Alpana runs for her life.)

Mom: Gigi! So now this for the expensive Catholic education?! Sommelier! I do not know.

She and many others thought it was just a phase that I was going through. It turned out to be a "phase" that has lasted for more than a decade. When something you're doing lasts for more than a decade, I think they call it a career.

Success with Wine, Success in Life

This book will be a success if it helps you learn how to comfortably order wine when with a date, boss or friends. It will also succeed if you go out after reading it and suddenly find how easy it is to purchase wine off the shelf for yourself, for guests, for party gifts—whatever.

Together we will demystify and enjoy wine. We will deal with wine and interpersonal situations that actually come up in all of our lives. In short, we will end up not just getting "a life"—we will end up getting a "wine life!"

Wine is not about expense, knowledge or snobbery. Wine is about personal choice. When you drink it, you know if you like it or not. Trust that. But first be totally open about drinking it. The personal and social rewards will be awesome.

Sugar & Spice

WINE AND THE SEXES

Sugar & Spice

If you're wondering why I chose to write a wine/lifestyle book geared mostly for women, it's because during my years as a wine pro it was pretty clear that women relate to wine differently from men. This does not mean that there is a solid gender-based difference: women and men do in fact enjoy many of the same wines. And contrary to some notions, women are certainly interested in developing their palates and their ability to select good wine.

Women are Cheap . . . No Way!

There are those in the wine industry who think we women are interested only in cheap, blackberry-flavored Merlot or wine's alcohol and carb content because we're more concerned about our waistlines than about good flavor. Granted, women are not as interested in the points or scores or the prestige of the product as men are. And that doesn't mean men are wrong to think that points and prestige are good reasons to enjoy wine. Women just use different tools to select wines. They are interested in what is immediately in the bottle, and they tend to drink wine for their own pleasure, without pretense or worrying about whether a vintage is less than desirable.

From the Alpana Files:
Women Rule . . . Wine

The New York Times reports that women purchase 77% of the wine bought in the U.S. and drink 60% of it. I think all the health and diet claims, ongoing media blitz and clever marketing definitely have something to do with this strong trend.

No Wine Snobs, Please!

There is a reason why the word "sommelier" brings up the image of a pompous, snooty male; why is it never the image of a pompous, snooty female? Could it be that women are less inclined to be wine snobs? Being a female in a male-dominated profession, I can't tell you how many times I've overheard men in full one-upmanship mode discussing wine allocations, points, prices and acquisitions. I think it's pretty safe to say that women are more emotionally connected to wine. I got into wine because it emotionally stirred me. For women, what matters most is the flavor of the wine and the story behind it and how wine can greatly enhance their social and private lives. There are of course a great many men who approach wine in a similar way, and I am hoping that they too will enjoy reading this book. But I have written on wine from a female perspective.

Wine Marketers Want Us Real Bad!

With *The New York Times* wine statistics mentioned above, it's no wonder that wine producers are scrambling to tap the female market. There's a new wine created particularly for women, a brand called White Lie. The vintner has gone to great marketing lengths to sell us on this concept, saying that White Lie is dry and light, with a lower alcohol content than other wines. It also has a series of stereotypical white lies stamped on the corks such as *I'll be home by 7* and *It's my natural color.* I wonder why they decided to lower the alcohol, since I don't think it's the alcohol content in wine that turns women off. Hey, I like to booze it up just as much as the next guy. Even though I don't agree with the idea of creating a lower alcohol wine for women, I decided to try the White Lie Chardonnay and, in all honesty, it wasn't too bad. As I do with all wines, I had to remain open to the possibility that I could like it. None of us, including wine experts, should ever judge a wine before giving it a fair shot.

Wine is the New Cosmo

If you haven't noticed, female celebrities are getting more and more into wine. A while back, I saw a video with Beyoncé holding a big glass of red as she laments and jokes with her girlfriends about a relationship gone South. Not so long ago she would have been crying into a Cosmo. With all due respect to *Sex and the City*, Cosmos are now very last century. Women are drinking wine, not fussy cocktails like appletinis.

Significantly, this shift in young women's drinking habits seems to have caught the attention of the entrepreneur Richard Branson, founder of the Virgin Group, who has recently introduced a Shiraz and Chardonnay, with screw top caps and even in mini-bottles, under the brand name *Virgin Vines*. He apparently "gets wine" and knows who's drinking it.

From the Alpana Files:
Wine vs Soda

The average American consumes 2.7 gallons of wine per year. The average American also consumes 220 gallons of soda pop per year.

We Haven't Come a Long Way, Baby, Quite Yet

While I'd like to be able to say that we're entering the golden age of women and wine, the truth of the matter is that, supportive stats or not, wine is still thought of as a male beverage. The stereotype that women don't know anything about wine hangs on for dear life. Unfortunately, women often buy into this inaccurate characterization. I repeatedly noticed during my sommelier days that women in the company of men seemed a little shocked when I asked them directly about their wine preferences. Some women, especially those in the early stages of a relationship, loved to pass the ego baton to the man and would say to me, "He knows what I like, talk to him about the wine." Those who have spent some relationship time together, and were more accustomed to joint decision-making, were much less shy about asserting their wine likes and dislikes.

When I was dating and the wine list was presented to my male companion, I tried to ignore this unfortunate *faux pas*. But this practice still goes on. To avoid this problem and open up the wine selection process, I believe both parties at a table should be given a wine list, so that couples can enjoy a few pleasant moments discussing wine. Of course, my fiancé lets me drive the wine choice—but I do discuss choices with him. Hey, do you tell the surgeon to sit there and look pretty while you do your own liver transplant? I think not!

I believe when a couple agree on a wine, both should be offered an initial taste. When, as a sommelier, I did this, women were often surprised. I responded to their reaction by saying, "Well, you're going to drink it, so I want to make sure you like it, too." Shouldn't everyone at the table like the wine?

Closing note to all servers and sommeliers: please include women in wine selection. Okay?

What Wine Can Do for You

There are many of us, and I used to be one, who have ill-conceived notions about what wines may be a good choice for ourselves, our friends, or significant others. We can start sorting things out and head in the right direction by getting to know what both men and women think about, or prefer in, wine.

From the Alpana Files:
Aging Wines

Waiting for Mr. Right vs. Enjoying Mr. Right Now

Believing all wines get better with age, many people will hold onto a bottle of a so-so wine. This is a bad assumption. Aging wine is kind of like a relationship. When you have good material to work with from the start, it can only get better. If at the beginning it's rocky, time can only make the situation worse.

Aging doesn't automatically make every bottle of wine better. Some poorly crafted wines have shelf lives shorter then a horsefly's. Other very good wines (too many reds and whites to even mention) are crafted to be enjoyed within a short time of being produced. There are lots of fun wines to be drunk right now. Talk to the wine pros at your favorite wine shop or restaurants to find out what you should age and what you should drink ASAP. Otherwise, while you're patiently waiting for Mr. Right, you may inadvertently be letting Mr. Right Now get away.

Women's Perceptions, Preferences and Notions about Wine

My female guests usually loved to know a wine's backstory before they made a selection, and for good reason.
Women usually don't have a specific idea of what wine they want. But they are interested when I can provide a wine's intriguing history. Women tend to relate emotionally and viscer-

ally to wine and the tales behind it. To a lot of us, wine is about passion, desire, romance, history and beauty—all conveniently and deliciously located in a glass right in front of us.

While fantasies clearly have their proper place, a true wine backstory can be fascinating, even inspirational. For instance, when women were heavily leaning towards buttery whites, I'd mention a terrific California wine called Marimar Torres Don Miguel Chardonnay. They became interested in this wine when I told the fascinating story of Marimar Torres, the daughter of Don Miguel Torres, a well-known Spanish vintner. Marimar wanted to break with tradition and be the first woman in the family to learn about wine-making, but Dad wasn't having it. After a few choice words with her father, Marimar took off for the land of opportunity and studied wine-making in California. She ended up creating her own winery and named her Chardonnay Don Miguel after her father. With the relationship repaired, on his deathbed Don Miguel told Marimar, "Yours is the finest Chardonnay I have ever tasted." Who doesn't want to try a glass of wine with that kind of inspirational story attached to it?

From the Alpana Files:
For a Party with Wine . . . Tell a Story

Anyone planning a wine-centered party should go on-line and pull up any interesting stories about the wine you plan to serve. Some wines have incredibly romantic stories of war, intrigue, opulent wealth, dashing noble-men and chaste beauties. Cut and paste the little histories onto homemade *cartes du vin* for your guests' amusement. Guests can then have a little laugh and get educated about wine at the same time!

Critics, Vintages & Points . . . Not So Important to Us

Women don't get so wrapped up in what the critics think, in a wine's vintage or even in how many points *The Wine Advocate*'s Robert Parker (considered by many to be the world's preeminent wine expert) may ascribe to a wine. But unfortunately, women sometimes allow themselves to be suckered into a wine choice because it is fashionable.

Flavor and Style

Women can actually be a little stubborn about their wine choices . . . especially when they want a wine from a specific varietal, a wine made from 100% of one grape variety. Varietals you may be familiar with include Pinot Grigio, Cabernet Sauvignon, Chardonnay and Sauvignon Blanc, to name a few. Women are more likely to drink Pinot Grigio or Chardonnay because they enjoy that particular grape's flavor. Style matters too: women would often perk up when I'd say a wine is buttery, oaky, light, dry or without a bite (a wine with low acidity).

When a wine is described as "dry," this sometimes means one thing to one person and something else entirely to another. "Dry" to some means oaky because they think that the oak is the dry flavor in the wine's finish or taste. To others, "dry" means the wine does not have obvious fruity flavors. When a wine professional says the wine is dry, he or she is referring to the fact that the wine has no residual sugar. It's important to clarify what it is you are looking for.

The descriptions "sweet" and "fruity" often confuse people too. Just because a wine is described as fruity doesn't mean it is sweet from residual sugar. I have seen guests shy away from a selection if I described it as fruity because they thought this meant the selection was sweet. Fruity refers to the fact that the wine has prominent fruit flavors such as tropical mangoes, juicy peaches, ripe Bing cherry flavors, etc. Wines that can taste fruity but are technically dry include Pinot Noir, Chardonnay, Alsace Riesling, Zinfandel and Pinot Gris. This is especially true if the grapes are grown in a warm climate. "Sweet" means that the wine has some actual residual sugar. Wines that have residual sugar include Gewurztraminer, German Riesling, French Pinot Gris and Vouvray. You can tell the difference between sweet and fruity by dipping the tip of your tongue into the glass of wine. Sweetness is detected at the tip of your tongue, therefore if you perceive a sweet flavor, the wine is residual sugar sweet. If you can't, then it is dry and simply has outstanding fruity flavors. As an experiment, try doing this with a glass of California Chardonnay and German Riesling side by side.

Quickies . . . Wine Varietals

As I said, *varietal* wine is usually made from 100% of one grape variety. California varietal wines qualify as a varietal even if made from as little as 75% of one grape variety.

The point to having a varietal is that you get a chance to enjoy a wine made with one dominant and delicious grape.

White Varietals

Chardonnay

One of the world's best-known white wine grapes.
MOUTHFEEL: Dry—Off Dry, Medium—Full Bodied
TASTES LIKE: Ripe Apples, Pears, Tropical Fruits, Buttery and Oaky
TIP: Chardonnay is a key ingredient in Champagne

Pinot Grigio

Crisp and vibrant white that is refreshing and easy to drink.
MOUTHFEEL: Dry, Light-Bodied
TASTES LIKE: Green Apples, Melon, Peaches and Lemon
TIP: Pinot Gris is the French synonym for Pinot Grigio

Sauvignon Blanc

Food-versatile and generously flavored white.
MOUTHFEEL: Dry, Light-Bodied
TASTES LIKE: Grapefruit, Citrus, Melons and Figs
TIP: California vintner Robert Mondavi invented the term
Fume Blanc as a synonym for Sauvignon Blanc

Riesling

Lively, fruity and fragrant wine also known as Johannisberg and White Riesling.
MOUTHFEEL: Medium-Dry—Sweet, Light-Bodied
TASTES LIKE: Apples, Peaches, Honeysuckle, Flowers
and Spice

Gewürztraminer

Difficult to pronounce but deliciously fruity and exotically perfumed.
MOUTHFEEL: Medium Dry—Sweet, Medium—Full Bodied
TASTES LIKE: Rose Petals, Lychee Fruit, Ginger and
Tropical Fruits

Reds Varietals

Cabernet Sauvignon

The most successful and popular of the top-quality red-wine grapes.
MOUTHFEEL: Dry, Full-Bodied
TASTES LIKE: Blackcurrant, Blackberries, Plums, Mint and Vanilla
TIP: Use a glass with a wide bowl to enhance the aroma

Merlot

Easy to love, Merlot is rounder and softer than Cabernet Sauvignon.
MOUTHFEEL: Dry, Full-Bodied
TASTES LIKE: Black Plums, Blackberries, Chocolate and Black Cherries
TIP: Drink this wine. Don't believe what they say about it in the film *Sideways*

Zinfandel

Exuberantly fruity and ripe, Zinfandel is America's Wine.
MOUTHFEEL: Dry—Off-Dry, Medium—Full-Bodied
TASTES LIKE: Raspberry Jam, Strawberry, Black Pepper and Baking Spice
TIP: The best Zinfandels are red, not white

Pinot Noir

One of the world's most elegant and sought-after wines.
MOUTHFEEL: Dry—Medium Dry, Light-Bodied
TASTES LIKE: Bing Cherries, Raspberries, Strawberries and Baking Spice

Gamay

Light, fresh and fruity red wine.
MOUTHFEEL: Medium Dry, Light-Bodied
TASTES LIKE: Strawberry-Banana, Pear Drop and
Raspberry
TIP: Gamay is best served chilled.

The Loving Language and Feel of Wine

We women are sensual creatures; this gives us an advantage in understanding wine because the language of wine is often very gender suggestive. Wine can be soft, velvety, smooth—so, who doesn't want a smooth guy?—regal, bold, sophisticated, an intelligent choice with a long finish! Women seem to love hearing these romantic Harlequinesque wine descriptions. So, when you are about to enjoy a great meal, realize you also become very susceptible to carnal suggestion. As you taste the wine, you will also *feel* the wine when the pairing with the meal is correct. This is chemistry at work . . . good chemistry.

From the Alpana Files:
Wine is Drunk at Warp-Speed.

Over 90% of the wines bought in this country are consumed within one week of purchase.

Wines Women Tend to Order

During my sommelier days, when dealing with a group of four women, I'd often think to myself, "Well, Alpana, time to start chilling the Pinot Grigio," and "Why even bother showing them a wine list?" This is because Pinot Grigio is *the* chic wine of the moment. PG's are very light, refreshing—carrying a water with a lemon slice flavor—and are eminently drinkable. Most importantly, PGs give you a decent buzz.

For the longest time, the hot wine with women was Chardonnay. With its butteriness and oakiness, Chardonnay is still very popular, enjoyed by women at happy hours throughout the land. Women have been influenced by clever Pinot Grigio marketing campaigns in women's magazines and on TV, and the result is that PG groupies have become part of what I call the Anything But Chardonnay, or A.B.C., movement.

Shiraz . . . the Girls-Just-Like-Me Wine

When women between legal drinking age and thirty-five who have interesting jobs but who need a roommate to afford to live in a cool neighborhood—they wear Ann Taylor and, if they have a car, drive a Passat—when these women want a red wine, they go for Shiraz.

Not only is Shiraz a pretty decent little wine, it often comes in at a reasonable $7–$8 a glass, or $8–$10 a bottle retail. Like me, the many women who drink Shiraz may also be watching their budgets. Women are more likely than men to drink a glass every day, and this wine offers a great chance to keep a nicely rounded day-to-day wine in the house.

I like to describe Shiraz as "sunshine in a bottle." It can really brighten your day and offers very little resistance in the way of tannins or harshness. Its soft, silky, over-the-top fruitiness makes you think that you're cheating on a diet because Shiraz can deliver a mouth-feel reminiscent of boysenberry pie filling. So if you're not careful, it can also trigger a craving for a scoop of ice cream.

Bottles of Australian Shiraz often carry labels with appealing graphics of animals. Pictures of adorable animals on a very recognizable varietal at a price under $10 per bottle, can make just about anyone want to buy an armful of this fun wine. This popular and highly drinkable wine offers solid bang for your wine-buck and gives you a chance to enjoy a little bit of sweet fruit from Down Under any old time you like.

Men Think About Wine... a Lot!

Men think about wine's structure, balance, chemistry, points, specific location and vintage. They seem less interested than many women in a wine that can spark an emotional response. I've noticed that male wine connoisseurs favor bolder, heavier wines full of tannins and girth; they are not intrigued by lighter wines that offer less heft and weight in the palate.

As a snapshot of the different ways in which men and women connect to wine, consider my future in-laws. Once I offered my wine-connoisseur future father-in-law a Spanish Rosé. He didn't like it. He said dismissively that the wine was "too easy to drink" and "there was nothing to ponder over." My potential mother-in-law however, used emotional adjectives, describing that same wine as "delightful" and "charming."

Now, before you point a self-serving finger at your boyfriend, lover, husband or father about their reasons for drinking wine, keep in mind that for every generalization I make, there are numerous exceptions. There are many men who truly enjoy wine for what it is—a tasty, organic, fruit-based libation!

From the Alpana Files:
Getting Over the "Pretty Boy" Phase

When I first became interested in wine, I enjoyed Chardonnays and Shiraz for the same reasons most women do. Like a sort of "pretty boy" object of desire, these wines don't ask you to think. You don't have to work too hard to enjoy Chardonnay's butteriness or Shiraz's berry-fruit jamminess. These wines are right there in your face, or in this case, mouth. These two wines were a lot of fun. But after a while, as will happen, my eye began to wander toward new, more adult and mature wine thrills. I was growing up and my taste buds had simply grown bored hanging with the pretty boys of wine. I needed the mental challenge of intelligent wines.

Fortunately, I developed an appetite for the more subtle and sophisticated wines like Cabernet Sauvignon, Riesling, Sauvignon Blanc and Sangiovese, as well as the urbane, wry and quirky Pinot Noir.

Next time you have your usual wine, stop and really think about the taste. Ask yourself, "Is the thrill still there?" If it isn't, it may be time to try something new that can meet the higher set of standards you are continuing to develop.

Men's Perceptions, Preferences and Notions About Wine

There are times when you may be going over to "his" place for a dinner he's cooking, or maybe meeting your guy pals for a steak dinner or treating your favorite uncle to a nice meal while he's in town on business. If you anticipate these kinds of social situations, it's probably a good idea for you to understand the relationship men have with wine.

Relationship-Saving Advice!

I don't want you to think that men and women have such huge taste differences that you can never enjoy wine together. In my days as a tableside sommelier, I observed many instances of peaceful coexistence between couples sharing a bottle.

However, there are times when wine is not quite working out between a couple. This often happens when a woman is with Bob the Wine Snob. You may know the type . . . while you just want to start the meal with a glass of something nice and light, Bob calls for an overpriced Cabernet Sauvignon just to show off.

The way to deal with Bob, and get what you want, is simple. While he's perusing the *carte du vin*, ask him to see if the sommelier or server can offer quartinos. You may know about quartinos: small wine pitchers that provide a bit more than one serving. Lots of places now offer this convenient wine service option. With a quartino you can start with an apéritif of a light white, and then move into the rugged wine territory where Bob can apply his impressive expertise.

While you are enjoying your quartino, tell Bob you'd love a taste of whatever manly vintage he has selected. Then he can tell the server to bring an extra glass so that he can personally pour you his special choice. With this maneuver you succeed in meeting the needs of both you and your companion.

Going quartino is also a pleasant way to increase your wine knowledge without bankrupting your date on something you may not like. By the way, everything here goes double if Bob is your father-in-law or boss!

If the restaurant doesn't have quartinos, go with something by the glass.

Men Drink Wine with Their Brains

Unlike Italians or the French, most Americans have not been raised to drink wine with lunch and dinner. So, as a result, many men decide to overcome their basic wine insecurities by developing a knowledge of wine in the same way that they improve a golf handicap.

They "learn wine" to improve their ability to entertain and impress social and business contacts. Time and again, I've seen men show off their ability to navigate a wine list in order to prove their sophistication publicly. They also look for expensive, high-profile brands. In short, they want a vintage Opus One for the same reasons they may want a Porsche.

A "Drink by Numbers" Game

Most men usually need a tangible point of reference to judge wine—a measurement, so to speak. Men love statistics and numbers; the point spread of games, batting averages and market quotients. Numbers are the gauge by which some men judge quality. Numbers can also provide bragging rights. For instance, one man may boast to another, "My '96 Barolo beats your '98!" Crazy thing is, this *mano-a-mano* bluster can go on even before the duelists have even tasted the wine they're discussing. The '96 owner believes that the vineyard's location, specific vintner and vintage will confirm his claim of superiority.

Performance Anxiety

Men sweat performance, whether it's V-8 engines, wines or their sexual prowess. If I mentioned that a wine was "Wine Spectator's Wine of the Year." or that "Wine Critic Robert Parker gave this wine 100 points," or that "This wine comes in a massive five-pound bottle with a six-inch cork," they would go for it like a fly to you know what.

Wines Men Tend to Order

Are you asking yourself, why do I care what wines men order? Let's see. If you know what they like, you will be better able to choose what wine gifts to buy or what wines to serve men in crucial business and social settings. Knowing what they like, you can steer them to wines you and your male friends, family and lovers can enjoy together.

Bar to Table

When men move to the table from having triple cocktails and beer belts at the bar, they want—no, let me rephrase that—they need big reds with their steaks and ribs. And men don't ask for their dressing on the side!

When I worked at tableside, the wine I saw men order over and over again was big, rich Cabernet Sauvignons or Meritage blend. They wanted that Napa Valley Cab full-bodied taste and feel. Because of their reputation as the "Rolex of Wines," Cabs have high prestige. This "Napa rep" makes Cabs the clear choice of many a man who values what's on the outside of the bottle—meaning the label—as much as what's inside the bottle. Another wine frequently ordered by carefully turned-out men is Brunello di Montalcino, a fine quality big, rich Italian red; they know it carries weighty prestige.

From the Alpana Files:
Sensual Talk

This may surprise you. Some men responded with interest when I compared wine with lingerie or a woman's body. If I said that a wine is soft, silky, well-endowed, voluptuous, and that if you give it time, it will open up, men seemed to get into it. What can I say?

Some Men Order Like Girls

When I've served men with more sophisticated palates, they often considered a lighter Chardonnay or Pinot Noir. While both of these wines, normally associated with women's tastes, are lighter in style, what they lack in structure they more than make up for in perfume. A great one of either of these will make a man, or woman's, heart swoon.

You Are What You Drink

PAIRING WINES & PERSONALITIES

Please understand, this isn't science we're about to explore. It's something I, and several of my sommelier pals, have noticed. Through our interactions with wine-drinking guests, close friends and intimate relationships, we have discovered that someone's wine choice reveals a lot about his or her personality.

You can have some fun with this personality and wine-matching stuff. Next time you're out with friends, pay attention to the wines they order, I guarantee you will not believe how on target this little insight is.

Que Chardonnay Es Tu?

There are two distinct types of Chardonnay. Most vintners manipulate Chardonnay so that it will have a buttery taste and oak flavoring, because wine marketers have convinced us that wood, instead of grape, is what you should taste in a glass of wine. Producers simply meet the mainstream expectation they themselves have created. So while those who like the buttery-oak Chardonnay are to some degree responding to a trendy and manufactured taste, I do admit to enjoying that Chardonnay personality because those who drink it are fun—buoyant and outgoing, and know what they like!

Across the Atlantic in Burgundy they're producing a very different interpretation of Chardonnay called Montrachet. (Chardonnay, as you may know, is the grape variety that is used to make white wines from Burgundy.) Montrachet is lean, crisp, has great minerality and, with little fuss, can stand out on its own. You might say that Montrachet drinkers are straight-forward and honest to a fault, unaffected by trends or what's considered "socially acceptable."

From the Alpana Files:
How Wines Are Named

To help you with wine-name confusions like the Chardon-nay/Montrachet sort of thing, you should know that American (also Chilean, Australian, Spanish, South African, et al) wines tend to be named after grape varieties like Zinfandel, Merlot, Syrah and Chardonnay. European wines are named after regions and places like Burgundy, Bordeaux, Chablis, Chateau-neuf-du-Pape, Rioja and Chianti.

Full Lives/Safe Lives

Like Chardonnay, with Riesling there is a clear line of demarca-tion between two personality types. To some, Riesling is Blue

Nun at a backyard BBQ—and that's fine, because the important thing is they're drinking wine!

But true Riesling fanciers find Pinot Grigio too neutral, Chardonnay too mainstream and Sauvignon Blanc too tart. They like Riesling because it has spine-tingling acidity and a fruit-and-aroma profile almost as complex as Middle East politics.

Riesling grapes are planted in inhospitable areas, like the severely cold and steep mountainside vineyards of the Mosel region in Germany. If you took the same grape and planted it in California, the wine these grapes make would taste flat and lifeless. The harsher the growing conditions, the better tasting the wine. Oh, did I mention that Riesling fanciers are also patient enough to hold out for the best? Good news for them, because Riesling is one white wine that gets great with age.

The Daring, the Tame, the Pink

Adventurous sensualists who are always looking for something new want Rosé, and they don't care what people think. They're the same sort of people who like sushi and/or sweetbreads. But Rosé is a much misunderstood wine. To explain, I need to borrow liberally from the observations of Bonny Doon winery owner Randall Graham, who once said Rosé drinkers are either "tragically hip" or "tragically un-hip."Meaning there are two types of Rosé drinkers: the hipsters who drink the trendy dry version and those who are wine illiterate and prefer the less cool sweet version, a.k.a. white zin.

The hipsters discover dry Rosés in the summer sun of Provence or Tuscany. These people also seek out the one place in their town that sells olives just like the kind they had with a Rosé in Nice. Sweet Rosé drinkers on the other hand are homebodies who are not knowledgeable about wine and prefer the sweet stuff. Many self-anointed wine sophisticates foolishly avoid Rosé because they think that only the "tragically un-hip" drink what they often jokingly refer to as "box wine." The joke is clearly on these wine snobs who denigrate all Rosé and think that just because it's pink, it must be sweet. Whenever someone ordered dry Rosé from me, I usually asked how he or she had discovered this much-maligned, but wonderful wine and then complimented them on their sophisticated tastes. Remember what I suggested earlier: no matter what type of personality you have, just be open to everything before you condemn it—you may be in for a real treat!

Red, White and Zinfandel

So, you're one who stands at attention for a Zinfandel, which is somewhat high in alcohol at 14–16%. This means you probably have an All-American personality. That stands to reason, because the grapes for Zin are grown only in North America. This wine is unpretentious and a serious party favorite. When you taste a Zin you can see that the wine's raspberriness, like our American culture, is totally extroverted. With Zinfandel, what you taste is what you get—right in the old kisser! I have to point out that the sweet White Zinfandel version has what I consider "bubble gum flavor" and is definitely not a sophisticated wine.

Is Beige a Color or a Natural State of Being?

One of the most popular wines in the U.S. is **Merlot.** It is a predictable wine, generally the same whether it comes from France, California or Italy. This is why the oenophile Miles in the film *Sideways* was so repelled by Merlot.

There is one Merlot that spikes out of the norm, and that is Petrus. Petrus Merlots are on many lists as one of the world's great wines. Petrus also tends to be rather expensive. Overall, Merlot drinkers are easy-going and they just go with the flow.

A God Among Mortals

Cabernet Sauvignon could be said to be the Katherine Hepburn or the George Clooney of wines. Cabs have great depth and substance with rich blackberry, full-bodied taste and feel. With Cabs you also get great lasting power, so the wine, which can be drunk young or old, ages well. When you read about somebody buying a $100,000 bottle of wine at auction it's usually from the Cabernet Sauvignon grape. The Napa Valley variety of Cab has great Bordeaux lineage. Cabernet Sauvignon reflects sophistication and natural elegance.

The Sassy Sophisticate

People who enjoy **Champagne or sparkling wines** tend to be *bon vivants*, devil-may-care types who want to enjoy life to the fullest. Their motto is "Life is too short!" They're downright manic at times, like Scott and Zelda Fitzgerald. Zelda, who was certifiably crazy, drank Champagne while she was riding around on top of Paris taxicabs!

From the Alpana Files
Champagne: the Bomb
Waiting to Go Off

If you plan to open a bottle of Champagne, or sparkling wine, it's all about SAFETY. First, keep in mind that you tend to open this wonderful stuff after you've had a few—which can add to the suspense, or body count, when you open it. Assuming the wine has been properly chilled in the fridge or an ice bath for an hour and a half, begin by having a cloth handy. Make sure the bottle is dry; you don't want this nuke to slip out of your hands as you defuse it. Next, remove the foil over the wire cage holding the cork in place. To give you some perspective—there's as much pressure in a bottle of Champagne as there is in a bus tire.

Next, take hold of the little handle on the cage and turn it six times to loosen it—but don't remove the cage. Allow the cage to rest on the cork and remember never to remove your hand from the cork once the cage has been loosened! This provides a little protection from what I call "premature ecorkulation." After the cage is loose, cover the top of the bottle with the cloth you have ready. Depending on whether you are right- or left-handed, hold the bottle with one hand from the dimple bottle bottom while with the other hand you hold the cloth covering the cage and cork. Keeping the bottle pointing away from people, pets or any valuable porcelain figurines, slowly twist the bottle while making sure the cloth/cork/cage area is stationary.

Amazingly, with almost no real effort, you will feel the cork slowly dislodge itself from its perch in the bottle's neck. If you've done this correctly, as the cork comes out of the bottle, all you should hear is a hissing noise. There should be no POP! Enjoy the bubbly!

Historical Note: Dom Perignon was not the inventor of champagne, as popular wine mythology would have it. What he actually did was introduce glass that was thick enough to keep Champagne bottles from spontaneously exploding.

Pairings

WINE, HOOKING UP AND DATING

Wine and the Lasting Impressions You Make

If you're obviously able to navigate wine selections, it will probably show both men and women that you are intelligent, and have both style and substance. Let's face it, if you're at a nice place and order beer and drink it from the bottle, you will make a very interesting impression. If you order a shot of tequila, it will make an entirely different impression. And, if you order a cocktail and use the hollow swizzle stick as a little straw, that will just look silly. Ordering a nice glass of wine says you're sophisticated. So follow along and see how socializing (a.k.a. dating, hooking up) and wine work together. We start right now with what a wine tasting can do for you.

Looking super hot in a really expensive dress can be immediately undermined if you order a diet cola. If you must have "soda" at a table about to be graced by wine, I suggest you have a sparkling mineral water. Anything but water, either sparkling or still, will ruin the wine's flavor. Also, if the entrees are more than $30 at a restaurant, don't ask what types of salad dressings they have unless you have an allergy. Pretty much assume it's going to be some sort of fancy oil and vinegar combo. Never ask to see if they can make a Caesar salad for you. And always order dessert. That dainty "I'm on a diet" speech is a total turn off—men like women who aren't afraid to eat.

Wine Tastings . . . "The" Social Lubricant

About 18 months ago, an actor known for doing Samuel Adams Beer commercials, was quoted in a major daily newspaper as saying about wine tastings, "I've been to these wine tastings, and they actually spit it out! We beer people actually enjoy drinking." If this person speaks for "Beer People" everywhere, there are a lot of folks who don't know what, or more importantly, *whom* they're missing when it comes to wine tastings.

While they may vary in expense and facilitator expertise, I believe that wine tastings are one of the best ways in the world for women from any number of backgrounds to meet men from any number of backgrounds. Plus, it's a pure and honest activity, because everyone attends knowing that it's all about drinking alcohol! Of course I'm kidding: it's really about having fun while getting a wine education.

Trunk Shows with Benefits and Few, if any, Creeps

Wine tastings, as I've already mentioned, are a great place to enjoy and learn about many, many wines. First, the cost is usually reasonable as you get to "try on" a lot of wines rather than going out and buying entire bottles of stuff you may not like. (If you think about it, wine tastings are a lot like designers' trunk shows.) Second, at tastings you are in the presence of professionals who can teach you about wine. Third, rather than having to reject a drink bought by a creepy stranger, at a tasting you can talk with anyone attending; it's socially acceptable and even expected that you be assertive with your co-tasters. Lastly, given a choice between meeting men at a happy hour or at a wine tasting, I say, "Bring on the wine tasting!" every time.

You may also meet someone at a tasting who wants to learn about a wine he or she knows nothing about, but you do. In this case you may be able to take that person by the hand, metaphorically speaking, and share your knowledge of a region and its wines. Mentor or lover, which shall it be?

Liberal Arts

Those attending wine tastings are often eclectic and intelligent, with a wide array of interests. It's a safe assumption that if people are into wine, they are also into food. If they are Foodies, they are likely to dig cooking, travel, geography, literature, history, films, music, theater and art—my God, they may even be that rarest of individuals: Liberal Arts majors! At almost every tasting I've ever been to, and that's a boatload, there's a little Renaissance spirit electrifying the air.

From the Alpana Files:
An Example of Drinking Wine
as a Humanities Class

If you ever have an opportunity to drink wine from the French vineyards of Mouton-Rothschild, take note: every year a different artist is commissioned to create the label of this world-class wine. Warhol, Matisse and Picasso are among the many famous painters who have been asked to do this. So as I sip a taste of Mouton-Rothschild, I not only experience the effect of wonderful-tasting natural science, but with the unique label I can see great art before my very eyes and learn some interesting history. More fun than studying the back of a box of Special K at breakfast, don't you think?

People who go to tastings are not from any one social stratum or career track; they often come from many different backgrounds. There's no other place I can imagine where you find surgeons, writers, stockbrokers, accountants, nurses, office workers, politicians and soccer moms together, all sharing a common interest.

Wine Tasting Your Way to Mr. Right

While you may not meet Mr. Right at a tasting, you may connect with Mr. Right's friends, relatives or parents. A parent is often a good indication of what the child could be like. One look at a father may provide a snapshot of a son. And as they say, sometimes the grape doesn't fall far from the vine.

Along with Potential Mr. Rights, Wine Tastings Are Everywhere!

You can find out about the millions (okay, a slight exaggeration) of wine tastings being given by checking online, looking at local newspapers, social magazines or even adult continuing education catalogs. Which means you can also find virtually every one of these wine-centered affairs.

Tastings are often held at wine shops and wine bars. Have some fun checking out—online or on the telephone—the wide range of wine regions and wine styles that retailers and wine bars may exhibit through a tasting.

Most of the time you can't beat wine tastings for site location. Tastings are often held at interesting, fun-to-be-in places, including cool restaurants, private libraries, chic hotels and intriguing museums.

Being Well-Traveled Can Make You "Wine Cool"

If you base your wine knowledge on travel experience—visiting California, for instance, or traveling through Europe—you can certainly interest people at wine tastings. Envision yourself saying, "I was backpacking through Avignon. For lunch, I picked up a great Cotes du Rhone, some tasty local cheese and fresh baguette. I ended up in a little park and shared the wine with some nice townies I met. We sat and watched people come and go for hours." This kind of story would prove to anyone that you're an intriguing, adventurous person with cultivated tastes.

Pre-Screening Advantage

Tastings let you pre-screen potential dates, because you know in advance that everybody there is interested in wine, so you have something to talk about. For instance, if you see a notice for a California Central Coast Wine tasting, and you have visited that region, chances are that people who go to that tasting may also have some connection with the region, so you have something in common right off the bat.

Wine Tastings and Speed Dating

Wine tasting has been around a lot longer than the 21st-century version of matchmaking called "speed dating." However, the fundamental principle behind these two highly social activities is the same. In both situations you must make a high-speed assessment.

In speed dating, you're in a room with a huge selection of suitors to choose from, a scene out of context from casual enjoyment. At the sound of a bell, you get three to four minutes to question and record your first impressions of each of a series of would-be boyfriends. The bell sounds again and you move, à la musical chairs, from one table to the next. You end by deciding which guys you would go to the ballgame with, take a romantic gondola ride with, introduce to your friends, go home with, get to know better or decide they're just out of the question.

At a wine tasting, you're in a room full of wines, a context with casual enjoyment. You get a little taste, maybe two ounces or less, of the featured wines. You record your first impressions of each wine. You conclude the evening by deciding which wines may be easy to drink with your upcoming dinner party menu, are affordable for everyday use, may impress your friends, are worth taking home to get to know better or are just a yuck.

Icebreaker

At wine tastings you focus on wine. Everything else you learn about those attending, or specifically a guy you may want to get to know better, is a really nice bonus. And you know, you can't beat an icebreaker like . . . "So, is that a well-structured, bold and powerful Rioja you're holding or are you just . . ." you fill in the rest.

Now Taste Wine!

Wine tastings make a great testing ground for many of the tips and tricks in this book. In particular, my theories about wine and personality pairings will be very helpful as you maneuver your way through a wine tasting. So, what are you waiting for? Go taste wine somewhere!

From the Alpana Files: Weird, But Oddly Accurate, Wine Descriptions

According to the French, wine is a food. As a fruit-derived food, wine easily lends itself to fun, tactile, vegetable, carnal and psychological descriptions. However, sommeliers often find it difficult to avoid describing wine as non-consumable objects. For instance, we're often tempted to say a wine smells like leather, a Barbie Doll (yes, some do!), a wet dog, cat pee, sweaty saddles, even goats. Our job is to filter these descriptions to something that sounds enticing. So, when you hear a sommelier or wine pro say a wine smells earthy or woodsy . . . this is a catchall for any non-consumable description-like leather, a Barbie Doll, a wet dog, cat pee, sweaty saddles or goat.

I have a friend who has an absurd, but telling, description of an indifferently made wine. After a taste of something indiscriminately and lovelessly manufactured, he'll calmly comment, "Hmm, it's an industrious little vintage."

Creating Your Own Wine Tastings

No party could be easier than a wine tasting. You can start either by providing all the wine or asking everyone to bring different wines to be served either in full sight, or blind (to create a little mystery, make sure all the bottles are covered with brown paper or fabric) based on any number of themes.

A **Book Club Tasting** is an excuse to get drunk and talk about the stuff you're all reading. Say you're all reading Arianna Huffington's trashy Picasso biography. Have the gang supply Spanish wines in honor of the great painter's country of birth. If the reading is *Under the Tuscan Sun*, the slam-dunk is Tuscan wines for everyone.

The **Wine Luck Party** has everyone bringing an ethnic dish from any of the major continents and a wine from the dish's place of origin. This party concept also has an added wine education component. It clearly demonstrates that wine and food from the same region tend to pair well. People can take this wine info and use it to select wines every time they go out to dine on French, Italian, Spanish and even American Regional cuisine.

You can also tie a **Wines from all Nations Tasting** into a world-class special event—like the Miss Universe Contest, for instance. Assign to everyone invited a wine-producing country that is represented at the pageant. As the pageantry unfolds, start pouring, and then proceed to complain about how skinny the women are and how much their plastic surgery must have cost.

Wine and Your Travels

Sharing first-hand travel and wine adventures is also an excellent way to motivate people to talk. This is an interesting way to find out if tastes and lifestyles of potential partners are compatible with yours. Let's say you find out he is interested in wine as you are. You continue to chat and learn he knows about food too. Then, if you're really lucky, you learn he knows his way around a kitchen. All I can say is, ding, ding, ding, ding, ding, jackpot!

From the Alpana Files:
Knowing the 6 Major Wine Styles

It took me six years of study to pass the Master Sommelier wine exam. I have spent thousands of hours poring through textbooks, memorizing facts, visiting wine regions, talking to winemakers and tasting countless wines. Through the course of my wine studies, I have found that most wines fall into six basic categories. They are light and dry whites, sweet whites, heavy whites, light reds, spicy reds and heavy reds. This categorization system is far easier to handle than memorizing the flavor attributes of the 45,000 different types of wine in the world. If you like a particular light white, chances are you will also appreciate something from the same category. So here, for your wine enjoyment, is a breakdown of the six major wine styles.

Light Whites: These are dry whites that are high in acid and light in body. They have the texture of non-fat milk and seldom feature oak flavors on the palate. The color is often pale yellow or straw-colored. The flavors are reminiscent of citrus fruit and although the aromas will differ from varietal to varietal, the general structure of these wines is similar.

Look for . . . Albarino, Dry Chenin Blanc, Gruner Veltliner, Orvieto, Pinot Blanc, Pinot Grigio & Dry Pinot Gris, Moscophilero, Dry Riesling, Muscadet, Sauvignon Blanc, Semillon, Soave, Torrontes and Dry Muscat.

Sweet Whites: Depending on the varietal, these are lighter-to-full-bodied whites that have a sweet flavor. The sweetness comes from residual sugar in the wine. The flavor and aromatics will differ from varietal to varietal, but most feature some type of floral aroma such as honeysuckle.

Look for . . . German-style Riesling, Alsace style Pinot Gris, Gewürztraminer, Vouvray style Chenin Blanc and riper Gruner Veltliner.

Heavy Whites: These are full-bodied whites with a whole milk mouth feel. The acidity in these wines is often low, while the texture is round, soft and silky. The color is often more golden and yellow. Most heavy whites have been exposed to oak. The fruit profile is ripe and reminiscent of baked apples and pears.

Look for . . . Chardonnay, Viognier and White Rhone Blends.

Light Reds: Light in body and color, these reds have low amounts of tannins. The light red's fruit profile is reminiscent of strawberries, raspberries and cherries. Depending on the growing region, these wines can also have mouth-feel. The color and tannins found in red wine actually come from the skin of the grape and not from the clear pulp on the inside. Just split open a blueberry. The juices on the inside will run clear but if you mash the blueberry between your fingers, you will see the color will leach out from the skins and stain the clear juice blue. Now imagine smashing a thinner-skinned Thompson seedless grape between your fingers. It won't be nearly as dark in color as the thicker-skinned blueberry. Each grape variety (Merlot, Cabernet Sauvignon, Syrah, etc.) has a different skin structure and flavor profile and the resulting color and texture of the wine will differ according to how thin or thick the grape's skin is. Some grapes like Pinot Noir have thinner skins; therefore the wines made from them will be lighter in tannins and color. The light red's fruit profile is reminiscent of tart red fruits like raspberries, cranberries, pomegranates and cherries. Even the light red color of the wine will remind you of these types of fruits. Depending on the growing region, they also have mouth-puckering acidity. These wines can also taste earthy with flavors of mushrooms, beets and fresh-turned soil.

Look for . . . Pinot Noir, Gamay, Sangiovese, Barbera, Dolcetto and Rosé.

Spicy Reds: These reds vary in weight, texture and body and, to state the obvious, are spicy in flavor. The fruit profile of the spicy red is often of riper or stewed fruits like boysenberry, raspberry or blackberry jam. These wines can have the aroma of black or white pepper, cinnamon, cloves, anise and other baking spices.

Look for . . . Zinfandel, Cotes du Rhone, Syrah & Shiraz, Amarone, Grenache, Primitivo and Pinotage.

Heavy Reds: Being full-bodied, dark-colored and opaque, with heavy amounts of tannins are characteristic of heavy reds. The finish of these wines, especially when young, will leave your mouth dry with a "fuzzy" coat. These wines will remind you of black fruits such as blackberries, cassis, blueberries, plums and vegetable flavors like black olives, green beans or bell peppers.

Look for . . . Cabernet Sauvignon, Malbec, Merlot, Cabernet Franc, Rioja, Tuscan Reds, and Bordeaux.

The Basic Four Points to Great Wine Tasting

What's really cool about wine is that it allows you, collectively or individually, to use all five of your senses to enjoy it. Hearing, sight, smell, taste and touch can all be brought into play to make wine drinking a sensuous experience. Oh, and if you think you can't hear wine, just think about how you feel when a bottle of Champagne pops open. If that doesn't get the old juices going for wine enjoyment you must be an alien!

Whether you plan to attend or give a wine tasting, here are a few tips that will help you understand how to get the most—beyond meeting Mr. Delicious—out of the experience.

1. Looks Are Important

Looks are important when it comes to wine. You can tell a lot about what's in your glass even before you smell it. So with wine, you actually can and should judge a book by its cover. Here's what to keep an eye out for:

- *White wines*—Come in a range of colors: straw, pale yellow, yellow, golden, etc. Wines from cooler climates will be more on the straw end of the spectrum and can sometimes have a green or silver tint. Warmer climate and older whites tend to have more of a golden hue with brass tints. If the wine is lighter in color, it will most likely be lighter in body and flavor as well, i.e. a pale straw-colored wine will be lighter than a deep golden-hued one.

- *Red wines*—Come in every version of red imaginable: ruby, garnet, red cherry, black cherry, violet, purple, maroon, orange, etc. Thinner-skinned varietals like Pinot Noir will be lighter in color, and thicker-skinned wines will have a deeper hue. Young wines will be more on the purple or indigo end of the spectrum, while mature reds will have a brown or brick-colored look along the outer edges. The greater the variation in color from the center to the edge, the older the wine.

- *Checking out "the Legs"*—Even before smelling wine, swirl the glass and you will notice "the Legs," the highly translucent streams of wine running down the inside of the glass. The number of legs you see gives you an indication of the wine's alcohol content (more legs can mean more alcohol) and a clue about what climate the wine is from. Since alcohol contributes body, weight and texture to the mouth-feel, you can get an idea of what kind of kick you may get from a glass just by looking at it.

2. The Nose Knows

How wine smells is really, really important, because 70% of
what you can learn about a wine comes through your sense of
smell. I really pity those who have had any kind of "probos-
cis remodeling" (I'm being so kind) because they may have
sacrificed interior olfactory surface area that could be used to
appreciate the astronomical number of wonderful ways wine
can smell!

- When the smell of wine is fruity it is described as
  fruit forward. If the smell is earthy (dirt) it is described as *earth forward*.

- If you smell wood, the wine probably comes from a
  barrel treatment of winemaking. The lack of a wood
  smell means the wine was probably made in stainless
  steel. Neither the presence nor the absence of a wood
  smell is any indication that the wine is good or bad.
  It only reflects the wine-making process. Some crafty
  wine producers throw wood chips into the process to
  lend the wine a wood smell or taste; they want you
  to believe it isn't wine unless it smells and tastes like
  the old oak tree in Grandma's backyard. Don't you
  believe that for a second!

- Wines can have a subtle smell of minerality such
  as chalk, wet slate or iron. From this you can guess
  in what part of the world and what type of soil the
  grapes of the wine you're drinking were grown.
  This soil guessing game can provide you a little
  fun while you're getting a buzz on.

3. Palate Effects

Okay, foreplay's over. No more looking at or sniffing the wine. It's finally time to go all the way and put it in your mouth. You can get a lot out of a small taste of a new wine because you can actually feel and become one with the wine (I'm from California, I can be a little flower-child-like now and then).

- Judging whether a wine is *dry or sweet. Sweet* is just that, a sweet taste. *Dry*, therefore, naturally means there is no sweet taste.

- You can use the "milk scale" to judge the *weight* of wine. Although wine is liquid, it can feel light or heavy. For a point of reference, you can use the feel of non-fat milk (light), 2% (medium body), whole milk (heavy), or half and half (really heavy) to judge a wine's weight. Whether a wine is light or heavy is no indication that it's good or bad, but it does tell you how to drink the wine or what to eat with it. Lighter wines make great cocktails. If a wine feels heavy and viscous, it belongs with substantial foods. This is pure, no-brainer logic: light wines go with lighter dishes, heavy wines go with heavier dishes. (More on pairing food and wines later.)

- The pucker-effect you may get when tasting, connotes the wine's level of *acidity*, which is the backbone of wine, and a naturally occurring aspect of it. If someone says she doesn't like "the bite" a wine has, that's acid doing a nasty to her tongue. Higher-acid wines can increase salivation making them perfect for salads with vinegar-based dressings. Wines from cooler climates will have more acid.

- Texture is an easy assessment to make the instant the wine hits your tongue and you roll it around in your mouth. Wine can be crisp, soft, coarse, rough or silky. For red wines you may encounter tannins which come from the skins of the grape or the oak barrel (wood tannins). Tannins will make the wine seem chewy and coat your tongue with a fuzz. If you want to experience tannins try brewing a cup of really strong black tea and drink it. That dry, grippy feeling in your mouth is caused by tannins. As red wines age, the tannins mellow out and become softer over time.

- As you taste, notice that there are many other flavors in the wine besides just the grape. The range of taste can be from apple to pear, from pineapple to lemon, from fig to melon, and can show up as a wine's *fruit flavor.*

- *Wood flavors* come from the barrels made from fine French or American oak. Barrel makers called coopers will char the inside of the barrels to give the wine more of a toasty caramel-like flavor. Winemakers can order their barrels with light to heavy toast depending on the flavor they are trying to achieve. You can tell if the wine was aged in oak if you taste or smell vanilla, toast, maple syrup, cedar, caramel, butterscotch, dill, coconut, cinnamon, nutmeg and other baking spices. American oak tends to give the wine more of a coconut-dill flavor while French oak gives off more of a vanilla quality.

- As wines can smell like minerals, they can also taste like them. Some of the more pronounced *mineral tastes* wines can carry include chalk, slate and iron. While not a bad thing, these mineral tastes provide a profile of the soil types in which the wine was grown. All the major wine-producing countries have regions where these mineral tastes can be found. You can find chalk, slate and iron in many Australian, American, Italian, French, South African and Argentinean wines.

- *Earth*, yes, wine can taste like earth. But earth is imbued with many wonderful tastes including mushrooms and beets.

- If wine gives you a bit of a *burn* in your mouth, it has a high alcohol content.

- You often hear the term *balance* used in describing the taste of wine. To determine whether a wine is balanced, see if any of the characteristics we've mentioned above are pronounced or are lost. If so, the wine does not have balance. When you can get a good combination of all these characteristics playing nice in your mouth, the wine is balanced.

4. The After Glow

Sometimes a wine's flavor is so fleeting that it vanishes as it heads down your esophagus. Other times, the flavor lingers pleasantly, like a cuddle after great sex. If you experience the first example, the wine has a *short finish*. If you experience the second example, the wine has a *long finish*. All the long finish does is let you appreciate the wine a few poignant moments longer.

Wine Dates that Travel Well

Okay, so you're at the point in a relationship where you can travel somewhere cool together. May I suggest that you consider one of the many fun and romantic wine destinations? Whether it's a reasonably priced weekender from Chicago to the vineyards of Michigan's Lower Peninsula or a blow-out-all-the-stops two-week wine adventure in South Africa, awesome wine locales are easy to find.

Wineries are, for the most part, close to some of the most scenic places in the world. With beautiful locations come good lodging and spa amenities; most importantly, you can probably count on delicious food at any vineyard because excellent produce often grows in or near wine regions.

If you prefer domestic travel, wine is now produced in all fifty of the states, including Hawaii. You can safely expect that there will be horseback riding, camping, boating, SCUBA diving, fishing, golfing—I repeat, golfing for the benefit of those who may need a way to leverage their golf-addicted partner to a wine region—skiing, hunting, off-road activities, and even some NASCAR tracks, near stateside locations.

These websites can help you find your dream wine trip

http://www.winecountry.com
http://www.greatwinecapitals.com
http://www.orbitz.com

You Don't Necessarily Get What You Pay For

You cheat yourself if you think an inexpensive wine (say $20 a bottle or less) isn't as good as an expensive one. This is because psychology can play directly into how we judge whether or not we like a particular wine. It's easier for people (even pros) to get a "Wow Factor" out of a less expensive wine because we expect less from a cheap wine than from an expensive one. Conversely, with a prestigious, high-priced wine, we tend to be more critical since our expectations are high to begin with. We expect more from a so-called (and oversold) "spectacular wine."

This brings me to my point. Once I went on a blind date with a man who, I was told, was a prominent, impressive, accomplished anesthesiologist. Wow! I knew I was going to be the wife of a successful doctor! My mother would be so proud! When he showed up, the reality was that he was considerably shorter than my 5'4", and turned out to be a real bore. Don't get me wrong: he was a nice enough guy, but in my head I had built him up, so I ended up being disappointed when he failed to measure up to my expectations.

With wine (as with blind dates) you should never go in with unrealistic expectations. Don't forget, with less expensive wines and attractive strangers, you should always be open to how pleasantly they may surprise you.

Date Troubleshooting: When Wine Becomes an Issue

As you may have guessed, I believe wine is the greatest thing in the world, that it can provide joy in many ways. Alas, sometimes this marvelous substance can generate issues between couples with different wine sensitivities, preferences and understandings. But fear not! Here are examples you may have experienced, where potential oeno-issues can be turned around to your advantage.

Handling Wine-Date Trouble-Makers— Surviving the "Wine Fetishist"

It truly pains me to say wine can sometimes become a wedge between people. Just as you can be a "golf widow" you can also be a "wine list widow." I have seen hundreds of women sitting at a table, lose their partner to a competitor made of high quality parchment and hand-tooled leather. I'm speaking of course of the wine list, the *carte du vin*.

Remember "Bob the Wine Snob" I mentioned earlier? He's the self-righteous oenophile who believes wine can't be appreciated without a degree and intense pretentiousness. Bob can ruin the enjoyment of wine for many a poor person who likes wine, but doesn't worship it. Wine, on the other hand, is not a passion to Bob; it's an obsession, a fetish. Wine Fetishists like Bob are compulsively narrow-minded and will believe wine media and points rather than trust their own taste buds to determine a wine's quality. When I had regular encounters with Bobs, they wouldn't even let me bring a taste of something unless it had the seal of approval from "the critics." Given the choice of making love to Angelina Jolie or drinking a '47 Cheval Blanc, Bob might well seriously think, "Hmm. You can always have sex."

Your response to Bob should be to insert yourself into his realm. Discuss what food you both plan to have or what he knows about the wines he's considering. Bite the ego bullet on this one and praise Bob's skills at picking that special vintage and then change the subject to something besides wine. You can always get back at him in the bedroom when you assign a point value to his love-making: "Gosh Bob, your performance tonight was adequate but a bit short on the finish. I give it an 85."

Surviving the "Wine Zero"

The opposite of a Wine Fetishist is the Wine Zero—that is, someone who has absolutely no interest in wine. If this happened to me, I'd dump the bum, but that may be a little extreme. What you can do with the non-wine fella is convince him that enjoyment of wine is manly. You should mention the masculine role models who own wineries. The ranks of "macho" wine producers include Heisman Trophy Winner Joe Montana, golfer Greg Norman, race car driver Mario Andretti, and filmmaker Francis Ford Coppola. Shoving all this testosterone in front of your man may jar him into giving a try to wine, the most natural thing in the world to drink!

It's a Bird, it's a Plane, it's the Wine Hero!!!

The antithesis to the *Wine Fetishist* and the *Wine Zero* is the *Wine Hero*. These were always my favorite people to serve. A Wine Hero is someone who is confident about, and devoted to, wine without the fanaticism of the Wine Fetishist. The Wine Hero cares less about vintage, points or press and more about tasting a great wine. He also has enough confidence to ask for advice, and the skill to do a quick check with his companions about what wines, flavors and foods they like before the sommelier or server arrives. These folks always made my job easier because they knew what data I needed to help them find the best choice, not just the most expensive or prestigious one. If you find a Wine Hero, he can be as much fun as a sunny day's ride on the back of Giovanni Di Italian's Vespa.

From the Alpana files: The Love/Wine Meter

The three easiest calls that I made about the status of a relationship based on what wine was being ordered came down to these:

Relationship Status: Hot new love
Wine Order: "Cristal for everyone!"

Relationship Status: Dying love
Wine Order: "We'll take the cheap wine from Texas, please."

Relationship Status: Locked in committed hate
Wine Order: "What can we get here by the glass?"
Exemplifying this last case, one guest actually said to me, "I would never drink what he drinks. Bring me a glass of the opposite of what he wants!"

What he orders says a lot about his dating intentions:

A bottle of Champagne: Casanova Alert! He's a smooth operator and he knows what gets the ladies going. Have fun and go along for the ride but just be warned that you're probably not the only woman on his speed dial.

Glass of Wine: Commitment Phobic! If he can't commit to a bottle of wine what makes you think he will commit to you? A bottle of wine takes a long time to drink but a glass of wine is quick and he's trying to tell you that he does not want the date to last very long.

Unless he's on medication or performing surgery the next day—BEWARE!

He asks you what you like first: Prince Charming!: You have yourself a real winner here. He cares about your needs first and foremost and takes an interest in knowing what you want. This is a very good sign and I would definitely make plans to see him again.

P.S. Never date a man who wears a blue tooth phone piece at all times, especially during dinner. Who wants to be with someone and know that you can be cut off for "an important phone call" at anytime? An evening with you is a special event and all other distractions can wait.

When You Like Zin and He likes Cab . . . Call on Dr. Singh

During my days as a sommelier, I had to act as combination marriage therapist/referee more times then you can imagine. I'm proud to say I kept quite a few couples from coming to blows over wine. The key to my non-accredited success at a table was to listen closely to both sides, and then come up with a wine that would satisfy everyone's taste. With 45,000 varieties of wine in the world (are you sick of me mentioning that yet?) there must be a wine that two people, claiming to have different tastes, will both enjoy.

The typical peace-making spiel I used sounded something like, "So, Madam, you like Zinfandel because you enjoy the brightness, jamminess and fruit forwardness. And you, sir, like Cabernet because you enjoy something with structure, earthiness and not too much fruitiness. I think I may have a wine that both of you may like." In cases like this, and this was a pretty typical scenario, I often suggested Spanish wines or something from France's Cotes du Rhone region. Both regions provide a lot of density, a little structure and some, but not too much, fruit. These two suggestions are also good with a wide variety of foods. Move over, Dr. Phil!

Here are some more compromises to help you avoid fairly typical head-on wine preference crack-ups.

You like: *Merlot*
He likes: *Pinot Noir*
Go for: *Sangiovese,* because it is lighter in tannins for the Pinot drinker and smoother, with a little fuller body for the Merlot fan.

You like: *Chardonnay*
He likes: *Sauvignon Blanc*
Go for: *White Bordeaux (Graves)* for the reason that Chardonnay drinkers usually want something big, rich and buttery while Sauvignon Blanc drinkers want the opposite, something light and crisp. White Bordeaux does the trick, because while it lacks the butteriness that Sauvignon Blanc drinkers dislike, it is heavy enough to satisfy Chardonnay drinkers, who will also appreciate the wine's innate oakiness.

You like: *Shiraz (Australian)*
He likes: *Syrah (French)*
Go for: *Syrah (Californian)* because it successfully mixes the smokiness of a Syrah with the berry fruit qualities Shiraz drinkers love. So, you basically get a smokey, blackberry taste. Isn't nature fascinating?

You like: *Sauternes*
He likes: *Port*
Go for: *Tawny Port (Portugal),* the ultimate compromise
wine. If you were to mix even parts of light-colored, honey-sweet Sauternes with dark-as-molasses,
plummy Port you would have Tawny Port.

With this helpful information, please consider your relationship officially saved. Taking into account the Asian-Indian
familial expectation that offspring will become physicists, engi-
neers or doctors. I think this couple's wine therapy qualifies me
for doctor status. My mother will be so thrilled!

Buy, Buzz & Bedroom

Before you come to blows with your partner over dry white
vs. light red at a wine shop, look for a wine seller to arbitrate.
Once you're done giving the personal preference data to the
wine seller, get some help to find a half-a-dozen different
bottles that may work for you and your partner. Take the selections home and do a little blind wine tasting. Cover the bottles
so labels can't be read, mix the bottles up so they all sort
of look the same, then arbitrarily start opening and
tasting. Through this fun little game, you may find new
wines that you can enjoy together. As a nice bonus, you
may get a buzz-on that leads to finding other ways to
make you forget what you were arguing about.

From the Alpana Files:
Sommeliers Must Play Tennis

Be certain when sommeliers discuss what wine you and a significant other may be having, that they listen to both of you. The most outward sign that they are doing this is if they look as if they're at a tennis match with their heads going back and forth as they listen to each of you. If the sommelier's head appears to be locked in place, chances are he or she is paying attention to only one player on the court, usually the side carrying the balls. If that's the case, make sure you step up to the net and lob in your opinion. Point, game and match!

Scenes from a Marriage

Working in a four-star restaurant for five years means you pretty much have a ringside seat at what happens between couples who are celebrating special occasions: birthdays, engagements and wedding anniversaries. You can't help but notice that the cadence of a couple's communications can change over the years, and that they can eventually morph into one being. I'll give you an example.

Let's start with a new young couple. At this stage of the relationship, the man clearly dominates the wine list. When I would ask what the two of them enjoyed in a wine, young men would respond with a barrage of "I" statements: "I like Cabs," "I like full-bodied this," "I like Bordeaux that," I, I, I, yi, yi, yi, yi, yi! Meanwhile, when I tried to ask the woman what she might like, the response was often a resigned, "Well, he knows what I like," accompanied by a giggle.

Same couple ten years later. The man still has complete control of the wine list, but he now says, "*We're* really into this wine because *we* visited this place and *we* liked it there." The pronoun "I" has been eliminated from his vocabulary. The woman happily defers to him while displaying her serious hand, "Oh that was such a romantic vacation where we got that wine!" Ahhh, she is beginning to have an effect!

Twenty years have gone by. The man still holds the wine list. He begins by saying, "*She* likes softer, lighter styles. I like this, but *she* likes that. And this is her special day." (Even though it's *their* anniversary, it has somehow become *her* day.) The woman laughs and says playfully, "Honey, that's not true. I also like the wine you like—you just weren't listening to me when we had that one wine together that we both liked, were you?"

By the time they reach the 35th anniversary, the woman controls the wine list. The man, while physically at the table, has mentally checked out. With little prompting, the woman goes into warp speed girl-talk with me. "We've got grandchildren who live in Oregon. You know they have lovely wines in Oregon, don't you? Their father always brings out these wonderful local wines when we visit, right, dear? My granddaughter said the most adorable thing to me the last time we were out there. You know she sips wine from her father's glass and she'll say, 'Nana, I like the bouquet.' Isn't that the cutest thing? Are you single, honey?" The man, having by now reached his saturation point, usually exclaims, "For God's sake, just order something!"

Peace and Love in a Glass

Throughout this chapter, I've encouraged you to have the wine retailer, restaurant server or sommelier help work out your differences in wine taste to a fun and often rewarding end. These folks have probably solved wine-preference dilemmas just like yours many times. So go to the pros for advice, and love wine together.

Wining & Dining

OUT OR IN

To Help Describe Wines You Enjoy . . .
Visit the Grocery Store of the Mind

Yes, I believe that the aroma of wine strongly suggests foods
of various kinds. So every time you smell a wine, take a quick
mental trip down the aisles of a grocery and think about what
food the wine smells like.

My educated guess is that for selections from the Light
White Category (see the basic 6 styles of wine) you'll find yourself thinking about things that are **green**. Lighter whites with
their pale straw color and aromas of tart citrus fruits have an
unripe element to them so the color green makes sense. Now
start thinking about grocery foods that are green: limes, hon-
eydew melons, green pears, green apples. Then again for the
light whites, you might also find yourself deep in the vegetable
aisles, surrounded by artichokes, green beans, green tomatoes,

arugula, bell peppers, asparagus and green herbs like cilantro and dill.

Selections from the sweet wine category will remind you of juicy ripe summer fruits like peaches, nectarines and apricots. You can also get into the exotic fruit and vegetable department where you will find ginger, lychees, star fruit, mangos and papayas. Wines from the sweet category will most definitely take you to the flower department where you will encounter the fragrant aromas of white flowers like jasmine, lilies, honeysuckle and gardenias.

Wines from the full-bodied white category have a riper element to them; therefore, the color **yellow** comes to mind. Unlike the light white category, the aromas are not as tart and citrus-driven and even the deeper color of the heavy-bodied whites tends to be yellow. For wines like Chardonnay and White Rhone varietals, you can call up the store section filled with ripe yellow fruits like ripe golden apples, yellow pears, pineapples and exotic tropical fruits like mangos and papayas. Other yellow items can be toast, butter and even apple pie from the bakery department.

The pale garnet, ruby color of wines from the light red category is reminiscent of tart red fruits, so think **red**. Wines like Sangiovese and Pinot Noir will remind you of tart red fruits like cherries, raspberries, cranberries, strawberries and pomegranates. You may also be reminded of earthy red vegetables such as beets.

Wines from the spicy red category will remind you of cooking spices such as white and black pepper, cumin and nutmeg. The fruit aromas will vary according to the grape variety, but the comment element tends to be riper fruits such as dried cherries, figs, juicy black plums, raspberry and blackberry jams. Don't be alarmed if the aromas take you down the condiment aisle where you will find soy sauce, liquid smoke, hoisin and

BBQ sauce. These aromas are commonly encountered with wines from the Spicy Red category. The scent and dark opaque color of heavier reds, like Merlot and Malbec may send you to the bins of darker black fruits so think **dark purple**. Aromas of dark purple fruits such as flavor-rich blackberries, black cherries, dark plums, figs and currants are often associated with wines from the heavy red category. Here are some other aisles of your mental grocery store that will connect with the aroma of wines:

Baking Section: Wines aged in oak will have the scent of items found in this section, such as cinnamon, clove, vanilla, nutmeg, molasses and nuts.

Fresh Baked Bread: The yeasty smell of certain Chardonnays and Champagne is like the warm bread produced from a grocery store oven.

Dried Fruits for the Holidays: Wines that come from a warm climate or have been aged well often smell like dried fruits including dates, raisins, prunes and cherries, that are placed up front at the grocery store during the holidays. Take Cabernet Sauvignon for example: when it is young the aromas may remind you of fresh black cherries, blackberries and plums. As the wine ages, the aromas go from being fresh to tasting more like stewed or dried fruits such as dried cherries and blackberry jam. The same happens with wines from warmer climates. The heat turns the grapes into raisins, so the aromatics of the wine will be more reminiscent of dried fruits.

Spices: Spicy reds like Zinfandel or Syrah are often described as having the flavor of black or white pepper. The intense and wonderfully pungent smell you experience in the spice aisle can be a lot like these wines. Mediterranean reds often smell like dried herbs such as marjoram, thyme or mint.

The Tea Aisle: This aisle can be extremely helpful in describing wines because the tannin quality, or astringency, given off by both the smell and taste of tea, is very similar to tannins in many red wines. Additionally, teas with hibiscus, lavender or rose hips can be compared to more floral style wines such as Gewürztraminer or Muscat. Some green teas duplicate the smokier nose and flavors found in red wines like Syrah and Cote Rotie.

Not Quite Out of the Store Yet

Now, while you're still at the Store, let the items you envision be your guide to what food you could pair a particular wine with. For example, if you smell lemons, think about what you put lemon on. A lemon squeezed on grilled fish is great, but you could also put lemon on fried calamari or grilled asparagus. Perhaps the wine smells like melted butter, which is often served with lobster, shrimp and popcorn. If you smell cherries, perhaps you could serve the wine with duck, which is often served with a cherry sauce. And, if you smell fennel, pair the wine with a dish featuring caramelized fennel. And if you smell bell pepper . . . well, you get the idea.

Animal, Mineral or Vegetable?

Being a sommelier isn't so much about telling guests what to drink, as it is finding out their preferences for all manner of things animal, mineral and vegetable. And it's not just about food with the wine; it's about relating a wine's basic features to someone's particular likes and dislikes. If, for instance, you hate plums, there are wines that go extremely well with a dessert, that I would never even mention to you. If I didn't know a guest's personal preferences, guessing what he or she might enjoy would be like a psychiatrist prescribing anti-depressants without ever having spoken to the patient. It's a bad idea to select wine without solid personal taste information. To uncover this critical information I had to relate quickly to my guests. The result for me and for you, if you use this method with lovers and friends, is to create a hand-in-glove fit between wine and drinker.

From the Alpana Files:
Taking Them from "I hate it!"
to "I love it!"

You'd be surprised how often people who say something like, "I am resolute. I hate California Chardonnay," will suddenly fall in love with a Chardonnay from Burgundy, France's cooler climate. The flavor of varietals like Chardonnay can be very different from region to region and country to country. I've heard many people say, "I hate Rieslings; they're all so damn sweet." But there are a lot of Rieslings under the sun. Some Rieslings from Alsace are much drier than the German-produced Rieslings, dry like a Sauvignon Blanc. I can't say this often enough: with wine it's a good idea to be open and flexible . . . just let wine happen.

Twenty Questions to Finding Good Wines

I used a variation of the Twenty Questions game when I was trying to find out the kind of wine someone might enjoy. Begin with the basics: "Would you like red or white? Something light or full-bodied? Something dry or sweet?" I then asked about favorite fruits, vegetables and spices: "Do you like cinnamon? Do you like oranges? Do you like licorice? Do you like asparagus?" I asked what scented flowers or potpourri they might like around the house, since wine preferences are so much about smell. This process helped me custom-fit wine to people's taste.

Ordering Wine in a Restaurant is Snap-City!

If you're hosting either a business or social event, you will want to appear to "control" the table, to show that you indeed "get wine." If you begin to sweat the prospect of ordering wine for others, fear not. Nowadays at most dining establishments, sommeliers and wine-savvy servers are on hand to help you through simple ways to order wine, ways that will both please and impress everyone in your party. I can pretty much guarantee that the following wine-ordering tips will leave your guests in awe.

For the sake of this discussion, let's say there is an available sommelier or a server very knowledgeable in the ways of wine.

Accurate Input Really, Really Helps

When everyone is first seated, gather as much information as possible for the server or sommelier. Find out, of course, whether those in your party like white or red, dry or fruity, light or heavy wine. If you discover that no one really cares what wine

to order, then, as host, you should go ahead and
order what you like, just as if you're giving a party
and supplying the booze.

Tell the sommelier what you prefer in the color
of wine and the quantity: full bottle, half-bottle, or
glass. It won't really help the sommelier or server
if you go into a long dissertation about low tannins,
hints of French oak, or that you don't want a wine with
a bite and so on. If anything, that may actually get
you into more ordering trouble because with this
approach you run the risk of confusing the somme-
lier. It's better to name a particular grape variety or a particular wine from your own wine preference list. Think about the
selections from the basic six styles of wine. Mention the types of
wine you normally enjoy, giving the sommelier license to bring
out something new and different. If you can't name a particular
wine variety, just ask for the basics, saying things like "I'm looking for a light, dry white wine," or "I'm looking for a full-bodied,
dry red wine." Again, use the basic six styles.

For Two . . . Super Cool and Easy

Many, many restaurants are now featuring a wide variety of
wines by the glass. If there are just two of you, ask the wine pro,
"Could you pair a wine by the glass for us with each course?"
This means that, from appetizers to desserts, you can have a
wonderful variety of wines without having to buy one or two
bottles to support every course of your meal. The reward is a
moment-by-moment wine-and-food adventure, as one glass
leads to another with a variety of fun taste results.

If you prefer, you can also hunt for the right bottle, or
bottles, to accompany your meal.

Four or More . . . No Cause for Alarm

If it is a group of four or more, don't worry about pairing the wine with everyone's individual courses. With even two bottles of wine, the odds are working against you to make pairing miracles happen. Instead, ask your guests which of them likes red and which likes white. If there's a fifty-fifty split, you will obviously need a bottle of red and a bottle of white. If you have a minority red or white holdout, you and the service person should help the holdout order something by the glass. Once you know what color, or colors, to order, rely on the service person to help you figure out consumption rates and quantity, so that you don't order too much of one and not another. Since pros see people guzzle all night long, they become pretty good judges about how much wine you'll need to make the evening a success.

From the Alpana Files:
The Wine Buck-olla$

The cost of wine does actually matter to all of us, maybe even if we're Bill Gates. Sixty dollars a bottle or more at a restaurant is a lot of money to me. I have access to some of the best wines on Earth, but I still live in the world of real budgets.

In the event you are not comfortable discussing price with your guests, call the sommelier over and ask him or her to look at the wine list from over your shoulder. As he or she looks with you, run your finger beneath the price, not the name of the wine—just a price you can afford and say, "I'm really looking for a red or white like this." If you keep running your finger underneath the price over and over again, your guests will think you're pointing at a particular wine selection rather than at the price. Pros get this message and without making you look like a cheapskate to your guests, they will help you get the best wine-bang for the buck you can afford.

The Most Food and People Friendly Wines

If you are faced with a wine list and don't know if the selection is going to pair well with everyone's palate and with what each person has ordered, then order a choice from the light white and light red category. Light whites such as Sauvignon Blanc, Pinot Blanc and Pinot Gris and light reds such as Pinot Noir and Sangiovese tend to be the most food and people friendly. You simply cannot go wrong with these choices.

When All Else Fails . . . Play the Champagne Card

If you can't get your party to agree on what wine to order, you can always play the *Champagne Card*. Champagne is the only wine that pairs well with almost anything you could possibly order and with every course of the meal; appetizer through dessert. The table staff will support this as a good and tasteful selection. Just remain open-minded and avoid any only-drink-Champagne-for-celebrations mindset. Plus, this little wine gambit will make you look pretty darn wine-savvy because few folks know this. You can expect a few to remark, "Champagne? What are we celebrating?" If this happens, simply explain the food/wine pairing flexibility that Champagne offers.

From the Alpana Files:
Tales of Lethal Champagne

During my days as a 21-year-old server at Montrio in Monterey, I set myself up beautifully for a major Champagne disaster. I had just removed the foil and cage from the top of a bottle of Champagne when something suddenly grabbed my attention. Stupidly, I walked away from a fully armed bottle of gas and liquid under pressure. You see, once you remove the cage from a bottle of bubbly, you are at the point of no return . . . you must remove the cork or suffer dire consequences.

As the minutes ticked by, the two guests who had ordered the Champagne realized that a time bomb resting in a wine chiller immediately adjacent to their table was about to explode. They could tell they were in imminent danger because the cork was slowly loosening itself from the bottle's grip.

Glancing back at the table, I wondered to myself why the couple were sliding lower and lower in their seats. Someone up there must have been watching over me because as I returned to the wine chiller, I casually picked up the ticking nuke, totally unaware of impending catastrophe, and the cork literally popped itself off into my hand; it really hurt. The two guests sighed in relief, and thanked me effusively.

Years later, when I was at Everest, one of my associates brought me a bottle of Champagne, which, while cool to the touch, had not been chilled enough to bring the contents down to a proper serving temperature. You

need to understand that Champagne at room temperature is more dangerous than you can imagine. In other
words, I had unwittingly been handed a rocket-propelled
grenade launcher with the safety switched off.

As I began to open the bottle, first removing the foil,
then the cage, the enormous pressure inside the bottle
pulled a Mount St. Helen on me, erupting with a force
great enough to launch the bottle into high-speed flight
right across the dining room. The bottle landed on a
vacant table and began to spin around like a Chinese
firecracker, spraying everything, and everybody, with
very expensive Champagne.

Figuring Out Wine Lists

When I was in elementary school we played a game called
"Hot Potato." Kids sat in a circle and quickly passed around a
beanbag, a.k.a. "hot potato," as fast as they could to avoid being
caught with it when the teacher called "Stop!" During my days
as a restaurant sommelier, I noticed that adult diners played a
similar game by quickly passing off the wine list to their dining companions to avoid being the one who was responsible for
selecting the wine.

Ordering wine at a restaurant can sometimes be a daunting
task and I certainly can't blame diners for wanting to pass the
responsibility for ordering to someone else. This is especially true
when one considers how many different types of lists one may
encounter: from one-page wonders to tomes the size of bridal
magazines. The key to making a wine selection easy and breezy
is first to figure out how the list is organized. Wine lists can be
organized in a number of ways: by price, color, variety, flavor,

region or simply in alphabetical order. So before you hand off the "hot potato" wine list to the person sitting next to you, follow my insider's guide to various types of wine lists and make a great selection; everyone at the table will think you are one hot potato.

Wine Lists as Big as the City Phone Book

When I was at Everest, the wine list that I maintained was eighty pages long with over fifteen hundred listings. Even for a pro, diving into the body of an enormous wine list can often cause data overload.

Occasionally, I noticed panicked diners flipping desperately through the wine list. Seeing this distress, I'd take a deep breath and head in for a wine-selection rescue mission. The lost souls would look up at me with glazed eyes and joke that the list was bigger than most phone books. While trying to avoid further embarrassment, I'd politely direct them to the table of contents. Like any book, most lengthy wine lists have a table of contents usually organized by a particular grape type or wine region. A good wine list table of contents will help you spot wines you've been hoping to try. You can also use the table of contents to ask your guests what wine they might like. Just read out some of the names to them from the list.

One other thing: once you find the wine you want, read the descriptive details carefully. You want to avoid the kind of mistake made by one of my diners. I had to point out tactfully that what he thought was the extremely good price of $27 for a Spanish wine, was actually the page number.

A Weighty Wine Issue

A common complaint that I hear from wine lovers is how difficult it can be to order wines at casual restaurants that don't have a sommelier or a wait staff who can offer proper wine guidance. In response to the growing requests for help in choosing wine, many casual restaurants now offer what are called progressive wine lists with wines organized by weight, flavor and texture instead of by grape variety. This approach gives diners some idea about the wines' flavor and characteristics without having to consult the server. If you see a particular grape you are familiar with, you will know that the wines listed in the same category are similar in texture and flavor, i.e. Cabernet Sauvignon listed with Malbec under "full bodied" or heavy reds. Some restaurants may also feature food graphics next to a selection to suggest a harmonious food-and-wine pairing.

The White vs. Red List

In wine lists using the "all Whites and all Reds" or "White vs. Red" format, wines are organized simply and effectively by wine color. This format can be manageable for the diner provided the list has only 40 or fewer selections. This list format may be broken down alphabetically or by pricing, neither of which tells you very much about the flavor of the wine. However, any White vs. Red wine list worth its salt will at least help you by listing the lighter wines at the top, with heavier selections nearer the bottom. Ask your server whether the White vs. Red list is progressive.

I'll take Priorat for $200, Alex—Working the Regional Wine List

The Regional Wine List is of course organized by a region or country of production. Unfortunately, these lists assume that everyone is a whiz at wine geography. Trying to make a wine selection from the regional wine list can be a lot like playing a version of the game show *Jeopardy*. The correct question for "Wines from Priorat" would be "What are full-bodied and intense reds made mostly from Carignane and Grenache grapes grown on mountainside vineyards near Barcelona, Spain?"

So regional wine lists are not very helpful unless you have some knowledge of the wine production areas and the types of grapes used to make wines in that region's flavor profile. I have come across regional wine lists that feature the backstory and history of each region and what flavors to expect. Reading these kinds of lists can be really educational and fun and it gives you something to do, especially if the people you're dining with are on the dull side. The good news about a regional wines list is that there's a very good chance it was put together by someone who really knows about wine and he or she may be in the restaurant to help you choose.

An Easy Wine Selection Geography Rule

If no professional assistance is available to help you select from the regional wine list, there is an easy way to remember a general rule of wine geography: *Wines made from grapes grown in cooler northern climates have more acidity and are not as high in alcohol as wines produced in warmer Southern climates.* For example, wines from Northern Italy are higher in acidity and not as fruit forward and robust as selections from the warmer Southern Italian wine districts. In the warm, sunny South, grapes will produce more sugar that converts to alcohol. With a higher alcohol content, wine from Southern Italy will be more full-bodied. Imagine what an orange would taste like if it grew in Minnesota instead of Florida. Don't forget that grapes are just like any other fruit.

A little addendum to this North/South variance is that wines produced in the coastal areas tend to be higher in acidity than wines from inland regions. That's because the cool breezes that come off the ocean temper the climate.

Pauillac is Not a Grape . . .
Good to Know European Wine Designations

To continue with the regional aspect of wine selection, most European wines are labeled and classified according to the region of production rather than the grape variety. The European emphasis on place names for wines evolved over thousands of years of growing grapes: wine producers have figured out where grape varieties will grow best. For example, in the wine region of Chablis, white wines are made from the Chardonnay grape, but this is not indicated anywhere on the bottle, the implication being that you should just know that Chablis is made from Chardonnay grapes.

The European producers' concept that region, and not necessarily grape, is ultimately more important in determining a wine's flavor is what the French call *terroir*, earth. Since geography is so important, many European countries have developed quality control systems to document and protect regional wine growing and production integrity. These systems include the French "AOC," the Italian "DOC," the Spanish and Portuguese "DO." Each of these are abbreviations for "controlled place names of origin." And they are most definitely controlled. To varying degrees, these abbreviations designate not only the boundaries which apply to each geographical region, but also a plethora of wine-growing and wine-making techniques, the type of varietals that may be planted in a region, as well as blending, growing, and harvesting requirements that producers must follow in order to use these geographical names. If you do see these designations on a wine list, it's a good thing because it means that a designated wine was created under very responsible conditions and conforms to high government standards.

The Regional Exception

Recently, a handful of Bordeaux and Languedoc producers started to put the grape variety on the label in addition to the region. This is intended to provide Americans with a cross-index, as it were. While it is unlikely that other European regions will adopt this practice anytime soon, this wise approach may help keep wines from Bordeaux and Languedoc in English-speaking markets. Until every regional wine includes the name of its grape variety, here is an at-a-glance reference to the more popular wines named for places and the grapes they are made from:

Region	White	Red
Sancerre	Sauvignon Blanc	Pinot Noir
Pouilly-Fume	Sauvignon Blanc	———
Macon	Chardonnay	Gamay
Pouilly Fuisse	Chardonnay	———
Burgundy	Chardonnay	Pinot Noir
Rhone	Viognier, Marsanne & Roussanne	Syrah, Grenache, Mourvedre & others.
Bordeaux	Sauvignon Blanc, Semillon	Cabernet Sauvignon, Merlot, Cabernet Franc, Petit Verdot & Malbec
Vouvray	Chenin Blanc	———
Rioja	Viura, Malvasia	Tempranillo, Grenache
Chianti	———	Sangiovese
Barolo/Barbaresco	———	Nebbiolo

NOTE: *Certain Italian appellations list the grape before the region: for example, Brunello di Montalcino, Barbera d'Alba, Moscato d'Asti. You can usually tell if this is the case if you see "di" or "'d" as part of the name. The other exception can be found with German wines, where the grape is often listed on the label.*

The Talking Wine List

A "talking" wine list is one that features wordy descriptions beneath each wine selection. Some of these can be vague, flowery and a bit like a real estate listing for a city apartment. You know the sort of thing I mean. When you see a place described as "cozy and charming with an updated kitchen and in move-in condition," it's only 200 square feet, and the landlord finally fixed the leaky sink. With that comparison in mind, remember the following "hot words" the next time you are faced with the talking wine list.

- *Elegant*—Don't expect too much body or flavor.

- *Refined*—The flavors have been so refined, you won't even be able to taste them.

- *Lingering*—The flavor of the wine will last and last, sort of like the scent of that CK One cologne we all used to think was so cool.

- *Robust*—Carries an alcohol wallop.

- *Impressive depth and richness*—The wine will cost more than your rent.

- *Hints of brambleberries, kumquats, vanilla and cedar*—Hope you like really intense potpourri.

- *Charming*—Often used to describe simple, less expensive wines. They will do the trick, but keep an eye on the price point; shouldn't be too high.

- *Aromas of a Provençal field on a warm summer day*— Wines that wax poetic often deliver short on promise.

The "Grape Variety" List

It seems to me that the most popular wine list formats I have come across are the ones that post wines by grape variety. In this type of wine list, wines made from the same grape variety are grouped together regardless of the region where they were produced. This means that a Sauvignon Blanc from New Zealand will be listed next to a Sauvignon Blanc from France. Even though two wines are made from the same grape variety, the flavor can greatly vary because of vintage, climate and wine-making style.

You can learn a great deal about wine from the grape variety wine-list format. You will learn the effect that vintage, climate and wine-making styles have on the same grape, thus increasing your wine repertoire. Try this: if you see a favorite wine, say a Pinot Noir from the Russian River area of Sonoma, on a grape variety wine list, have a Pinot Noir from another area and see how the flavors compare. It's very likely that you'll end up discovering another wine you'll like for entirely different reasons.

Visiting Enotecas . . . Raising the Bar on Wine

I generally avoid over-hyped nightclubs and bars; I like the romantic and relaxed environment of wine bars, or as the Italians call them, *enotecas*. Just a few years ago it was *eno-whaa*? These days, it seems an increasing number of wine bars are popping up in almost every metropolitan area of the country. Wine bars actually date back to Roman times when busy citizens would stop by the local enoteca to join friends for a pre-dinner snack and a refreshing glass of wine at the end of a hard day trading chariots or whatever they did for a living back then. The modern enoteca encourages a similar spirit of pairing and sharing and usually features a "small bites" menu with a very nice array of wines. These fashionable temples to wine may come across as trendy and nouveau chic: they usually offer elegant surroundings and sleek Euro designs. I do believe that the popularity of wine bars will last considerably longer than the Disco era.

Enotecas are not just for hardcore wine buffs. They are great places to learn about wine in a relaxed and un-intimidating atmosphere while enjoying the company of friends. You are also likely to encounter like-minded people who appreciate discovering and learning about wine at one of these fun places. So the next time you and your gal pals are looking to paint the town red, I suggest you ditch the long lines at the clubs and head for your neighborhood wine bar. Best of all, there's no cover charge and you don't have to worry about some drunken Vince Vaughn wannabe spilling his vodka and Red Bull on you.

Having a Glass of the Tasty, But Unpronounceable

The wine selection at enotecas can sometimes be obscure and quite foreign. This is not a place to order your standby glass of Chardonnay. You will encounter wines from all over the world made from different types of grapes, some of which can be tricky to pronounce. I'll admit it, I still recognize only half the choices on some enoteca wine menus. This small and sometimes challenging inconvenience does, however, offer a great benefit; it allows me to learn about new wines and wine regions.

As you should, I tend to rely upon enotecas waitstaff to guide me through the unique offerings. Unlike other types of restaurants, at enotecas the waitstaff are often well-educated in all matters wine. A savvy enoteca server can be like your own personal wine tutor. After a brief discussion with you about your tastes and preferences, the staff should able to suggest the right wine, maybe share a fabulous story about the selection and recommend the best nosh to go along with the choice. Gotta love enotecas.

I get asked all the time, "How can I learn more about wine?" I usually respond, "By drinking it." No book, vintage guide, magazine, expert opinion or website can ever substitute for putting the liquid into your mouth. By offering sample portions of wine, enotecas present plenty of put-wine-in-your mouth opportunities. I really think you lose out if you don't try more than one wine during your enoteca visit.

When Portion Control is a Good Thing

Wines at enotecas, besides being ordered by the glass, can often be ordered in one of three ways: in two-ounce tastes; by the quartino (a charming little glass pitcher holding roughly a third of a bottle); or by the mezzo litro (another attractive glass pitcher containing about half a bottle). If you come in a group, you can order a number of quartinos or mezzo litros. By sticking to the smaller two-ounce wine portions, you can experiment with various small-plate entrees. It's fun to see how different wines change the flavor of food, and vice versa.

The Flight Path

Many enotecas also feature wine flights. A wine flight is a selection of three to six wines served in two-to-three-ounce portions. The enoteca staff will select the wines and arrange them according to a common theme—grape variety, country, vintage or flavor. Often, with the flight, servers will present little cards with descriptions and facts about the wine choices. These mini-wine tastings are a perfect way to learn about wine by allowing you to compare and contrast one wine with another. Within a flight, there may be a wine or two that might be out of reach economically if served alone. The good financial news is that one price is generally attached to all the wines making up a flight. This allows you to spend less on a variety of wines than if you had the same wines served in full individual pours or by the bottle.

Understanding the Enoteca Menu

Enoteca menus are often inspired by the cuisines of Italy and other Mediterranean countries like Spain and Portugal. Since enoteca portions are small, they provide an opportunity to try many different food selections. I recommend starting off with olives and cold appetizers such as salume or antipasti, then moving on to sandwiches or hot food and finishing up with cheese and desserts. Here are some of the more popular dishes to be found on enoteca menus.

> *Antipasti*—Antipasti comes "before the meal" and refers to small snacks, usually of vegetables. They are intended to stimulate the appetite.

> *Crudo*—Crudo means "uncooked' or "raw" and usually refers to delicate slices of raw fish served with olive oil and sea salt.

> *Panini*—Panini, or "little breads", are grilled Italian sandwiches usually made with vegetables, cheese and grilled or cured meat.

> *Cichetti*—Cichetti comes from the Italian word "nibble" and represents various "finger foods."

Fritto—Fritto is "fried." Fritto Misto, or lightly battered, is a fried mix of seafood, meat and vegetables.

Affetatti—Affetatti or "slices" refers to various types of cold cuts like mortadella, prosciutto, salami or bresaola.

Salumi—Salumi is a single word that describes Italian-style cured or preserved meats like salami, sausages or pate.

Fromaggi—Fromaggi is cheese.

Having Him . . . to Dinner

If you're seeing someone nice, and want to invite him to a home-cooked meal, make a fun game out of discussing favorite flavors and smells with him before he comes over. If you find out that he likes Granny Smith or Winesap apples, you can go to the wine shop and talk to the pros about your dinner guest's preferences. How good is it going to be when he sips a Graves from the Bordeaux region with the bay scallops you've slaved over and says, "Wow, green apples! You know I love green apples!" Score! Of course this works with family and friends too.

She Handles her Man

We have established that having solid personal taste information is crucial when selecting wines for others. It can sometimes even be a marriage saver. I can best explain with a non-wine example. I have a friend whose wife, we'll call her Jackie, hates cigar smoke, but once a year she graciously allows him to smoke in the house. But there's a catch; Jackie gets to choose the cigar. She goes to a good cigar shop and rattles off all her husband's likes and dislikes in food and drink to the professional cigar sellers. The cigar guys then take great pains to show her several selections that she will be able to tolerate, while satisfying her husband's preferences. It always works like a charm. This has become a tradition and Jackie's husband looks forward to every Christmas. This clever lady also uses this technique to pick out wines for the two of them, and for family and friends. No *garbage in/garbage out* in this example; Jackie provides the experts exactly what they need and everyone wins.

From the Alpana Files: Wine-a-romatherapy

As I mentioned earlier, wine is 70% about smell. To help you increase the range of wines you and others may enjoy, I've created the following Wine-a-romatherapy list below. It simply presents smells many of us get off on with wines that have the same smell characteristics.

So, if you like the smell of . . .

. . . apples—you'll like Vouvray.

. . . raspberries—you'll like Zinfandel.

. . . honeysuckle—you'll like Viognier.

. . . candle wax—you'll like Semillon.

. . . a roaring fire—you'll like Pinotage.

. . . the sea—you'll like Muscadet.

. . . evergreen trees—you'll like Retsina.

. . . eucalyptus—you'll like Shiraz.

. . . cinnamon—you'll like Grenache.

... fresh cut grass—you'll like Sauvignon Blanc.

... bacon cooking—you'll like Cote Rotie.

... fresh herbs (parsley, sage, rosemary & thyme)— you'll like Sauvignon Blanc.

... toast in the morning—you'll like Champagne.

Wine and Business Entertaining ... Looking Like a "Rock Star"

Probably the most important aspect of successful business entertaining is to make sure you control every detail of the event that you can. When I was a restaurant sommelier, I can't tell you how many times I saw those who were entertaining for business, wasting the opportunity to impress an important business associate. In most cases, all that was needed was a little pre-meeting planning before the critically important business luncheon or dinner.

Here are a few thoughts, related to wine and, in general, that will help you have a business entertainment success.

Find Out What Wines the Guest Likes

If you are in a position to do it comfortably, call the executive assistant/secretary of your business entertainment guest and ask what sorts of wine your guest enjoys. You'll be surprised how much personal preference information these "office sergeants" can share about their bosses. Refer back to my *Twenty Questions* section earlier in this chapter for what to ask.

From the Alpana Files:
Guests Don't Select!

When you foot the bill for business or personal entertaining, it is appropriate that you select the wine. A key reason for this is that the last thing you want is for your guest or guests to worry that the wine they select may be too expensive or incorrect with the meal. You want your guests to be happy and comfortable, not sweating any details.

Talk in Advance to the Venue

Once you have your guest's personal preference info, call the restaurant and speak with the sommelier, wine director or general manager. Give them the data so they can help you make an advanced wine selection. If you're feeling confident—as you should from studying this book night and day—let them know the possible selections that you want on the table when you get there. If you're entertaining on a "corporate decreed" budget, don't hesitate to let the restaurant staff know your cost pain threshold, then and there.

Incidentally, always, always do business entertaining at a restaurant you know well. Why take a chance at a place you don't know? Additionally, if in any way a restaurant seems resistant to helping you create a successful business entertainment experience, cross it off the list and check with another place. You can't afford to lose clients because of a botched meal.

If you've done your homework and advance planning, you might want to have, rather than a wine list, the sommelier or server bring to the table, the guest's preferred wine, saying, "Good evening, Mr./ Ms. So-and-so. We have been informed that you prefer this '02 Chateau Blah-blah-blah. Please enjoy." You'll look like a rock star when this happens! If the guest turns to you and says, "How did you know I enjoy the '02 Chateau Blah-Blah-Blah?" just smile and say, "I have my sources."

When There's No Advance Wine Ideas

If you can't find out what wine your business guest prefers, talk to the restaurant staff and establish a price point in wines that you can choose from. This will prevent a potentially anxiety-making wine list being brought to the table. Also ask that a nice sparkling wine be at the table when the guests arrive. This is an extremely sophisticated move.

Cover the possibility that your guest may not care for sparkling wine, by having on hand a white and red by-the-glass choice that could be effortlessly substituted by the service staff. You can avoid what could be an uncomfortable moment, and at the same time look both in control and highly attentive to your guest's needs.

Easy Food & Wine Pairing

So far I have done my very best to make enjoying a lifestyle that includes the pleasure of wine drinking as fun and easy as possible. Now I'm going to suggest a way to pair food and wine successfully.

This method will help you match the flavors of wines and foods in a way that, while general in nature, makes logical sense. To paraphrase the famous adage, "When you give someone a fish he eats for a day; teach someone to fish and he eats for a lifetime." With this pairing method, "fishing" for the right food/wine pairing will become easy as pie. Snap quiz time! What wine would you pair with pie? For the correct answer, read on!

Out With the Old Rules

The old, outdated rules of pairing red wine with meat and white with fish or poultry are just that: old, outdated rules. Pairing rules have changed because more and more restaurants are serving fare that is global or fusion, where ethnic cuisines are combined, or "fused," in style. An example of food cultural diffusion might be Chicken Curry Quesadillas, a dish that intermingles poultry, mild cheese and spices from two distinct cultures. All this crossover cooking is not happening just in the largest cities where you can find places serving everything from Indian-Mex to Franco-Japanese dishes, it's happening everywhere.

From the Alpana Files:
Confessions about Pairing

Before you suffer from apprehension or anxiety about this food/wine-pairing thing, memorize the following quote from Jancis Robinson's book *Tasting Pleasures, Confessions of a Wine Lover.* It will give you reality perspective on pairing:

"I think that for every dish there probably is one perfect wine, but that for most of us, life is too short to work out what it is."

The Supreme Pairing Concept . . . New Rules

If you can remember only one thing from this book about pairing wines with food, this is the most important concept I could possibly share with you: *Compare or contrast the most significant taste feature of a dish with the most significant taste feature of a wine.* This is the real trick to making successful pairings between virtually hundreds of food choices with hundreds of wine choices.

Applying this supreme pairing concept, I came up with a way that good pairings can happen, using the familiar tastes anyone can find in everyday foods and food condiments. Some may say the following food/wine pairing matrix is radical thinking. I say, sometimes the simplest ways to do things are the best.

For wines in the light white category the condiment factor is lemon juice. These wines can be paired with any type of food you would squeeze a lemon on. From salads to oysters, the zingy acidity is a great complement. The weight of these wines will also pair well with foods that have a delicate preparation such as steaming or poaching.

The condiment factor for a sweet wine is of course sugar. The sweetness can be used to complement sweeter sauces or it can be used to counterbalance the effect of spicier ones. Wines high in residual sugar also provide a great contrast to salty dishes.

Heavy whites offer great texture and weight therefore they can be paired with heavier dishes featuring rich cream or butter sauces. In the case of Chardonnay, the condiment feature is butter. Chardonnay can easily be paired with foods that are served with drawn butter.

It is also important to consider how the food is prepared and this is one of the reasons why old school rules like "red wine with meat" are so last century. If I tell you to select a wine to go with a piece of steamed fish, then a lighter white wine may be an appropriate pairing. But what about a piece of fish that has been marinated in spices and then grilled outdoors? A lighter white would still work, but it would not enhance the smoky and spicy flavors. A selection from the light red category or the spicy red category would be better choices to match the effects from the marinade and cooking technique. But, in the end, it's your call. Now isn't it nice to be free from having to follow outdated rules?

Lighter reds are usually higher in acidity; therefore the comparable condiment is red wine vinegar. Vinegar is often used to cut through the fattiness of oilier foods. Similarly, wines from the light red category can be paired with oilier fishes such as salmon or tuna as well as richer meats like duck or sausages. You could also choose to match the wine's acidity with tangy items such as tomato sauce (this is why Chianti and tomato sauce work so well together; you are matching a high acid wine to a high acid sauce). Light reds also offer the most versatility when it comes to food and wine pairing. Because they are low in tannins you can pair them with traditional "white wine friendly" dishes such as lobster or corn chowder.

Wines from the spicy red category are perfect for dishes that are cooked with spices. Imagine how well the peppery quality of a Zinfandel or Cotes du Rhone will pair with a peppercorn-crusted filet. Spicy reds are often robust and packed with jammy fruit flavors, so they will handle dishes that are braised, grilled, smoked or cooked for long periods of time. If the preparation of the dish includes tons of spices, any wine from this category will complement it.

Heavy reds often feature intense flavors of blackberries, cassis, plums and other dark fruits; therefore the comparable condiment is a rich red wine reduction. You can pair these wines with any food item that will go well with a red wine reduction, meaning beef, lamb and game. One of the reasons why heavier reds are paired with meat is because of the similarities in texture. A chewy wine works well with chewy meat. A heavy red also works well with any dish that has been cooked or braised in red wines, like stews.

As you can see, the possibilities are endless when it comes to food and wine pairings. You will find that two very different wines will work extremely well with the same dish. One may highlight the texture more while the other will enhance the spice flavors. There really is no right or wrong answer. The most important thing to remember is that you should first and foremost drink what you like, experiment and have fun with your food.

LIGHT WHITES

Albarino, Dry Chenin Blanc, Gruner Veltliner, Orvieto,
Pinot Blanc, Pinot Grigio & Dry Pinot Gris, Moscophilero,
Dry Riesling, Muscadet, Sauvignon Blanc, Semillon,
Soave, Torrontes, Dry Muscat

Condiment

HI ACID = LEMON JUICE
Pair with any food with squeezed fresh lemon.

Texture

Crisp & light bodied

Complements

Food Texture	Anything crispy & crunchy
Tangy Flavors	Vinaigrettes, tomato-based sauce, cocktail sauce, white wine sauce, tartar sauce, feta or goat cheese, pickled foods, citrus-flavored sauces, yogurt, sauces with pungent olives, capers or anchovies
Green Foods	Herbs, asparagus, green beans, Brussels sprouts, artichokes, leeks, pesto, broccoli, bell pepper, peas, lettuce, etc.
Salty Flavors	Soy-sauce-based sauces & marinades, pate, cured meats, cheese, smoked salmon, olives, nuts, cheese
Lighter Meats	Chicken, pork
Seafood	Lobster, oysters, shrimp, crab, octopus, mussels, squid, clams, oilier fishes
Cooking Method	Poached, steamed, boiled & sautéed & deep fried

SWEET WHITES

German Style Riesling, Alsace style Pinot Gris, Gewürztraminer, Vouvray style Chenin Blanc & Riper Gruner Veltliner

Condiment

SWEETNESS = SUGAR
Pair with spicy foods to reduce "heat" or to compliment sweet sauces.

Texture

Will vary according to the wine.

Complements

Sweet Flavors	Sweet & savory fruit sauces, sweet & sour sauce, sushi rice, candied nuts, sweet salad dressings. relishes, chutneys, sweet peppers, root vegetables, peas, corn
Salty Flavors	Soy-sauce-based sauces & marinades, peanut sauces, cured meats, cheese, smoked salmon, olives, nuts
Spicy Foods	Mexican, Indian, Thai and Chinese cuisine, chili pepper flakes, black pepper crusted, Wasabi paste
Tangy Flavors	Vinaigrettes, tomato-based sauce, white wine sauce, lemon sauce, pickled foods, citrus-flavored sauces
Honeyed Meats	Glazed hams, honey-roasted turkey, BBQ chicken
Seafood	Lobster, shrimp, crab, octopus, squid, raw fish, unagi, scallops, oysters, mussels, clams

HEAVY WHITES

Chardonnay, Viognier, White Rhone Blends

Condiment

MOST CHARDONNAYS = BUTTER
Pair with anything served with drawn butter.

Texture

Full bodied & soft

Complements

Food Texture	Pasta, creamy soups, meaty textures
Creamy Flavors	Butter & cream sauces, cheese sauces like Mornay, Alfredo or cheddar, coconut milk, mayonnaise, hollandaise sauce, brown-butter sauce, creamy dressings like ranch & 1000 Island
Sweet Flavors	Sweet & savory fruit sauces, relishes, brioche, chutneys
Foods Served w/Butter	Corn, sweet potatoes, lobster, crab, fish, scallops, shrimp
Meat & Meat-Like	Chicken, turkey, pork, beef & mushrooms
Cooking Method	Breaded foods, sautéed, grilled, roasted

LIGHT REDS

Pinot Noir, Gamay, Sangiovese, Barbera

Condiment

TARTNESS = RED WINE VINEGAR
Pair with tangy sauces or use to cut through richness of fattier foods.
Versatile style of wine.

Texture

Light-bodied with soft tannins

Complements

Food Texture	Meaty textures
Sauces	Tomato-based sauces, red wine reductions & marinades, red fruit sauces, cheesy dressings like blue cheese
Earthy Flavors	Mushrooms, truffles, beets, turnips, parsnips
Herbs & Spice	Dill, oregano, sage, thyme, tarragon, rosemary, basil, black pepper, anise, cinnamon
Salty Flavors	Soy-sauce based sauces, cured meats, black olives
Fatty Foods	Chicken, pork, lamb, duck, goose, Ahi tuna, salmon, Mahi Mahi, swordfish, cream sauces, cheese, cheese sauces like Mornay, Alfredo or cheddar, sausages & pate
Cooking Method	Grilled, sautéed, pan-seared, smoked, BBQ & broiled

SPICY REDS

Zinfandel, Cotes du Rhone, Syrah & Shiraz, Amarone, Grenache, Primitivo, Pinotage

Condiment

SPICINESS = SPICE BOX
Pair with foods cooked in spices or braised and grilled foods.

Texture

Medium to full bodied. Tannins vary according to wine.

Complements

Food Texture	Meaty textures & hearty stews
Herbs & Spices	Black pepper, anise, Indian & Mexican spices, cinnamon, dill, thyme, sage, rosemary, oregano, tarragon, cumin, jerk seasoning
Sweet, Tangy & Spicy Sauces	Teriyaki sauce, BBQ sauce, ketchup, maple syrup & honey glazes, stewed fruit reductions, red wine reductions & marinades, peppercorn sauce, tomato-based sauces, mole sauce, enchilada sauce
Salty Flavors	Soy-sauce-based sauces, semi-hard & hard cheese, cheese sauces like Mornay, Alfredo or cheddar, cured meats, black olives
Meat & Game	Chicken, turkey, pork, lamb, duck, goose, venison, meat loaf, steak
Cooking Method	Grilled, sautéed, pan-seared, smoked, BBQ, broiled & braised

FULL BODIED REDS

Cabernet Sauvignon, Malbec, Merlot, Cabernet Franc, Rioja, Tuscan Reds, Bordeaux, Barolo & Barbaresco

Condiment

INTENSE FRUIT = RED WINE SAUCE
Pair with foods that are prepared with a rich, red wine reduction.

Texture

Medium to full bodied. Velvet soft to chewy tannins.

Complements

Food Texture	Meaty textures & hearty stews
Red or Brown Sauces	Savory fruit sauces, red wine reductions & marinades, tomato-based sauces, Madeira & Port sauces, gravy & au jus
Herbs & Spices	Dill, oregano, sage, thyme, tarragon, rosemary, black pepper
Salty Flavors	Semi-hard & hard cheese, cured meats, black olives
Earthy Flavors	Mushrooms, truffles, beets, turnips, parsnips
Fatty Meats & Game	Lamb, sausage, cured meats, beef & steak, meatloaf, corned beef, venison
Cooking Method	Grilled, seared, smoked, BBQ, broiled & braised

Un-wine-ding

RELAXING WITH WINE;
TIPS ON BUYING TOO!

How do you end your day? Most of us have seen the soap commercial in which a model-perfect businesswoman comes home to her lush apartment, to be happily greeted by her loyal golden retriever. She slides gently out of her Manolo Blahniks and her couturier suit to do a perfect triple gainer into a Mediterranean-sized tub.

The whitening toothpaste commercial presents the same "perfect" woman (this chick gets around!) heading after work with her elegantly coiffed gal-pals to a favorite spot where the men are all Eric Bana-esque, wearing well-tailored Ermenegildo Zegna.

To my mind, one thing is seriously missing from these two idyllic Madison Avenue moments—a good glass of wine! We can take a little time here to talk about relishing the moments when you get to kick back and relax and how those moments can be made ever so much nicer with wine.

My soft landings, at home or play, are a little different from the two mentioned above. When I get home, the first thing I do is kick off my scuffed Nine Wests. Then I drop my mail on the nearest flat surface, along with my keys, messenger bag and the Thai takeout I just bought for dinner. I head into the bedroom to hop into something with an elastic waistband before I trudge into the kitchen to see if there's a bottle of wine already open in the fridge. Then I plop onto my cushy couch, and eat the food and drink the wine, while I reflect on the day I just survived. After that, indulging in a nightly guilty pleasure, I turn on the tube for some VH1 celebrity dish, *The Soup*, or catch up on Tivo'd Jon Stewart (a great pairing of both smart and hot).

If I do go out with the girls, it's usually for just one nice glass of wine, because I'm exhausted and have to get to bed early to rest up before I begin the whole life-work cycle the next morning.

From the Alpana Files:
The "Chill the Cheap Stuff" Trick

For the wine I drink at home, I rarely spend more than $15 a bottle. If it's a special occasion, I splurge. For the most part, though, I'll save the money to spend on more important things—like shoes. I know a little trick that will make an inexpensive wine taste more impressive: simply chill it. I recommend that you use this ploy if you choose to serve inexpensive wines at your party: you can make the "off" flavors of a cheap bottle of white disappear by popping it in ice for 15 minutes. The same technique when applied to reds will make them taste earthier and richer, eliminating the high-tone alcohol flavors that can taste metallic or "tinny." The other benefit to icing down the wine is that the glasses resting in your guests' hands will warm up more slowly, again masking the taste of an ordinary wine for a longer time.

Home Alone?
A Chance to Focus on Wine

As a teenager, I was always bewildered by the '70's TV sitcom moms who knocked on their children's bedroom doors before entering. In our household, privacy was nonexistent. In addition to entering our bedrooms with no hesitation, my mother often used a public address system to page both my brother and me; she had an extremely loud voice.

A lot of this "open door policy" was the result of Mom seeing one too many *Dateline* episodes about teenagers doing "the drugs." She assumed that a locked door meant my brother and I were up to no good. She insisted that anything I wanted to do alone, I should be able to do in front of the family. Needless to say, I never had a quiet time alone at home until I moved to Chicago and into my first apartment.

I remember how quiet it was the first time I came home to an empty apartment after a bustling night at the restaurant. At first, it was not so much every tiny noise I could hear that was frightening, as much as the idea of being alone. To calm my nerves, I popped in a Sade CD and poured myself a glass of wine. The moments that followed were a complete revelation. Just as the stillness in my place amplified every sound, the flavor of the wine I was drinking was amplified too. Every single flavor component of the wine seemed delightfully heightened, distinct and more delicious than usual. It wasn't that the wine had changed, but rather that with so few distractions, my attention was more focused. As Sade crooned about a "Smooth Operator," I gradually succumbed to the relaxing charms of the smooth operator I was holding in my hand.

As I discovered, when, for whatever reason, you are home alone, your senses are heightened. The absence of the constant din created by people during your commute, at work, at the gym or by hand-held electronic distraction—what I call life-noises—allows your senses to easily refocus on smell, taste, color and texture in all things. Some of the things that you are suddenly more aware of can be the feel of a silk robe, the scent of those wonderful bath salts you brought back from an Arizona spa, the sight of a wavering candle flame, or the rapturous taste delivered by a special wine.

I think society tells you that there is something wrong with you if you are by yourself. While I know a lot of people don't like the thought of being alone, I have come to cherish the time that I spend by myself. That's why when you're alone it's a great time to do the things you enjoy or wish to do.

Now, I don't want to get into any trouble with people saying Alpana is promoting drinking alone. I am emphatically not saying that. What I am saying is, you may want to take a pleasant little journey away from it all with a really nice glass of good wine when you are alone.

From the Alpana Files:
Wine as Therapeutic Release

Things you start to think about when you're alone and the wines that will help you relax, justify and forget.

- My ex-boyfriend got engaged before I did!!! *Fat Bastard* Chardonnay (France)

- I'm up for review and I hope I get a promotion and raise. *The Money Spider,* Roussanne-d'Arenberg, McLaren Vale (Australia)

- I've been meaning to organize my closet for months. *Wits End "The Procrastinator"* Cabernet Franc/Shiraz, McLaren Vale (Australia)

- I'm attracted to a co-worker and he doesn't know I'm alive. *Obsession White Wine* from Ironstone Vineyards (Sonoma)

- And then I followed him home the other night because I wanted to know where he lived. *Therapy* Pinot Gris, Therapy Vineyards (Canada)

- I've been dating the most amazing guy for the last three weeks and he is perfect! *Head over Heels* Cabernet/Merlot, Berton Vineyards (Australia)

- I just found out he has his profile posted on ten different dating websites and he still logs on. *"Goats du Roam"* Red (South Africa)

- I just found the most awesome dress and boy, do I look hot in it! *Glamour Puss* Pinot Noir, Cooper's Creek (New Zealand)

- I don't care if my apartment is a mess, my bills are overdue and I can't fit into my pants anymore, I'm still an articulate, stunning, gorgeous, amazing, talented, super fabulous woman. *Goddess* Pinot Noir, Mundrakoona Estate (Australia)

Time for Simple Complexity

So what do I drink when I'm enjoying time by myself? Complex wines are what I drink when I'm away from all the life-noise. This is the time when you can focus your senses on the flavors delivered by wines like deep, brooding, richly textured reds that change flavor as they open up.

You can also enhance the high-end wine experience pretty easily with a little Coldplay or Jill Scott playing on the iPod deck, a glow from the fireplace and a good book. This is like a spa treatment for the mind, without the massage.

From the Alpana Files:
What Wines Go with Bingeing?

You just broke up. You're bingeing.
As you gorge yourself on . . .

. . . **potato chips** and uncontrollable sobbing, have some **sparkling wine** or Champagne.

. . . **pizza,** you can also curse his horrid name and the wretch he threw you over for while you smack your lips over a **Zinfandel** (it's high in alcohol too!).

. . . **Hagen Das Pralines 'n' Cream Ice Cream** and realize this is all somehow for the better, pour yourself something nice and sticky like a **Sauternes** or **Late Harvest Muscat.**

A Chance to Pamper Yourself

You pamper yourself with facials, manicures, pedicures and Hagen Das every now and then. So why shouldn't you pamper yourself every now and then with wine? Being alone gives you a chance to experiment with the good stuff. The next time you're off to your favorite wine retailer to buy for others, sneak a really, really good bottle in for yourself. Go for something you haven't tried before such as a

. . . bodacious Bordeaux like *Chateau Lascombes Margaux*

. . . seductive Burgundy *like Marquis d'Angerville Volnay "Les Caillerets"*

. . . toasty Champagne like *Krug Multi Vintage*

. . . racy German Riesling like *Dr. Loosen Urziger Wurzgarten Spatlese*

. . . gorgeous Pinot Gris like *Weinbach Cuvee Laurence Alsace*

. . . too good to share Chardonnay like *Kistler Sonoma Coast*

. . . smoky Rhone like *Jean-Michel Gerin Cote Rotie*

. . . robust Italian like *Allegrini Amarone della Valpolicella*

. . . intense Spanish like *Alvaro Palacios Finca Dofi Priorat*

. . . suave Californian like *Lewis Cellars Cabernet Sauvignon Napa Valley*

This "solitary wine exercise" will provide a chance both to pamper yourself and learn a little more about wine.

From the Alpana Files:
Solitary Activities Paired with Wine

- *When listening to '70s and '80s Pop Music,* try Rhone wines with a spiciness that goes well with any upbeat tempo.

- *When listening to Classical Music,* try something heavy, rich and traditional, like a Bordeaux.

- *When listening to Top '40 Music,* try Merlot—the plummy fruit quality appeals to a wide audience.

- *When listening to Hip Hop Music,* do a Malbec full of deep brooding fruit that matches the lyrics created from personal street experiences.

- *When reading "Chick Lit,"* try Pinot Noir, a delightfully feminine wine with seductive perfume and silky texture.

- *When watching Reality TV,* try a Riesling, The wine's acidity pairs well with the contempt and hatred the contestants have for one another.

If It Stirs the Emotions, It Can Be Paired with Wine

I've talked a lot here about one of the five senses that can stir some of the most powerful memories and emotions: the sense of smell. This is the most important sense for enjoying wine because if you can't smell wine you can't taste it. (Duh.) I believe that anything in the world that elicits an emotional response can be paired with wine: flowers, scenery, literature, great art, a sunset, architecture, music, clothes, even movies—all can be paired with wine.

So logic dictates that when you combine the aroma of a particular wine with watching a favorite movie at home, the result can be a very pleasing and intense emotional experience. To further illustrate the power of combining aromas and movies, an inventive Japanese company has created a new movie-going experience that combines scents cued to be released into the theatre during certain movie scenes. When moviegoers see a scene enhanced by this technology—say in a lovely garden, they then experience the smell of fresh flowers and grass, making for a complete sensory experience certain to elicit emotions.

The good news is that we don't have to go all the way to Japan to experience a variation of the emotional experience this *smell-o-vision* technology provides. Anyone can replicate it right at home, in a fun and decidedly low-tech fashion using only a well-chosen bottle of wine and a DVD player.

Junk Food and Wine

Wine can be drunk with virtually any food, even good old junk food. For your fulfillment and appreciation, below are some of my favorite "guilty pleasure" meals and snacks teamed up with fun wines.

Breakfast

Egg McMuffin & Mimosa—One of the benefits of waking up at the crack of dawn is that you can order breakfast at McD's before the "no exception whatsoever" 10:30 a.m. cutoff. I recommend going with the "breakfast wine cocktails of champions," the festive Mimosa. The Champagne OJ combo adds both wake-up tartness and bubbles that will balance the Egg McMuffin's sinful richness.

Lunch

Grilled Cheese 'n' Tomato Soup & Barbera d' Asti—This classic comfort food was one of my first lessons in pairing a beverage (soup, in this case) with food. As a kid, I loved the way the soup's tartness cut through the creamy, gooey American cheese. The Bing cherry tartness of an Italian Barbera d' Asti will work the same magic, only with an added wallop for us big kids.

French Fries & Prosecco—Have you ever noticed how certain foods like M&Ms, potato chips and french fries somehow taste better when you steal them off someone else's plate? I also think that the calories of these pilfered foods don't count when you get them this way. Anyway, I like to eat my french fries dipped in an equal mix of ketchup and mayonnaise, or as I call it, Alpana's Franco-American Aioli. A Prosecco is the wine that goes well with my special dipping sauce, because it cuts through the fries' salty richness. Say, if I drink my Prosecco from somebody else's glass, does that mean the wine's calories don't count?

Lunch or Dinner

Lean Cuisine Fettucine Alfredo & Macon (or Pouilly Fuisse)— When I eat a Lean Cuisine Fettuccine Alfredo, I am reminded for some reason of the joke used in the opening scene of *Annie Hall*, where two women are complaining about a Catskill Mountain resort's cuisine. One of them says, "Boy, the food at this place is really terrible," and the other one answers, "Yes, I know! And such small portions!" Anyway, the green-apple tartness of a simple French Chardonnay like a Macon or Pouilly

Fuisse is a better match to cut through the richness of the cream sauce than a big, buttery California Chardonnay. The cuisine is lean; therefore the wine should be lean as well.

Fried Chicken & French Champagne—A few years ago I attended a backyard summer party featuring nothing but fried chicken and Champagne. I thought I had died and gone to heaven. There was fried chicken as far as the eye could see and a kiddy pool filled with ice and a seemingly endless supply of Champagne. Everyone had a piece of fried chicken in one hand and a glass of bubbly in the other. The tartness of the Champagne helped cut through the fat of the chicken. It was pure unadulterated delightful decadence.

Mac 'n' Cheese & Beaujolais—Whether it's the low-fat TV dinner version or the kind that comes out of a box, Mac 'n' Cheese is the ultimate comfort food. When I was a kid, I loved strawberry soda with my Mac 'n' Cheese for the same reason I enjoy the fruitiness of well-chilled Beaujolais with the dish. Beaujolais mimics those nostalgic flavors perfectly.

Snacks and, if you're willing to admit it, Dinner from time to time

Cheetos (Baked) & Zinfandel—My favorite junk food is Cheetos, and I would like to personally thank whoever invented the baked version. Now I can enjoy my favorite snack with 40 percent less guilt. Anyway, the robust fruitiness of a Zinfandel is a perfect match for the orange chemicals that cover the Cheetos and stain your fingers for a week.

Artichoke Spinach Dip in the Bread Bowl & Pinot Grigio—There's just something irresistible about a good 'n' creamy spinach dip. It must be the fact that it comes in an edible bowl.

I love it when I can hide incriminating evidence by eating bowl and all. The crisp lean texture of a perfectly chilled Pinot Grigio will provide a delicious contrast to the creaminess of the Artichoke Spinach dip. By the way, do you know if this dip counts as a vegetable serving? Just curious.

Ranch-Flavored Rice Cakes & Austrian Gruner Veltliner—If you have ever been on a diet, and who hasn't, I'm sure you've limited your daily intake to gallons of water, numerous carrot sticks, cans of plain tuna and styrofoam chips, er, I mean rice cakes. I recently spotted a ranch-flavored version of the boring rice cake and thought; hmmm, this is most definitely an epicurean oxymoron. I purchased a bag and washed the cakes down with a bottle of Austrian Gruner Veltliner. It turned out to be a delicious pairing. Not only did the wine help moisten the cake's texture, but the wine's pepperiness actually enhanced the ranch flavoring; it was like adding freshly ground pepper to a garden salad with ranch dressing.

Seven-Layer Bean Dip & Pinot Gris—No casual party is complete without the ubiquitous seven-layer bean dip. The mark of a great bean dip is that no two bites should ever taste the same. Some bites feature sour cream, while others exude guacamole and/or cheese. Whatever the taste, the dip's texture should be smooth with a spicy flavor. The slight fruitiness of Pinot Gris tones down the "heat," while the roundness of the wine complements the soft textures of the dip.

Buying Wine For Moi!

Have $100 to spend on yourself? You do? That's great, because a great way to spend it is by visiting your favorite wine shop with a good idea of what wines you'd like to try. Once you're there, let them know you have a budget of $100 for only five or six bottles.

Since, as I said, part of my wine education was gleaned in a Carmel, California wine shop, I know how retailers think. Right off the bat, they're going to lovingly take extra good care of you because you're buying five or six bottles of wine. Usually they end up spending twenty minutes with people wanting only one bottle for $15.99. Trust me, you'll be considered a prize.

With your budget and the number of bottles desired firmly established, take a couple of minutes to fill the retailer in about your wine preferences. Once you've done the wine data download, ask to be provided with a range of wines from a light white to a heavy red—and you're all set

The Wine Connection

Another really cool way to buy wine for yourself is to talk to a favorite wine steward, sommelier or beverage manager and tell them how much you appreciate their wine knowledge and selections and you want to know where they go to buy wines for their home. Once they stop enjoying the compliment you just tossed them, they should provide you a name of a store. Since you're a good customer and one who appreciates the wines served there, you may go on to ask a favor. Would they mind arranging an appointment for you to go to the wine retailer to buy a few bottles of wine? Chances are they will say yes— folks in these restaurant beverage positions want to take good care of their chosen wine retailer, their "wine connection."

So the appointment is made and "highly referred" you show up with $100 cash in hand. When you meet the "wine connection," you once again, as with any other wine professional, fill them in on your personal tastes, what you've recently tried and liked or disliked: do the whole wine preference thing. (NOTE: You don't go into a car dealership and say, please sell me a green car. No, you very definitely declare your many personal preferences. This same approach is needed for this buying excursion.) In all likelihood, since you are a preferred customer of their contact at the restaurant, the wine connection will allow you to try the goods before you select any wines in their collection. Not too shabby, right?

Back at Home . . . Sampling the Wine

You're now the proud owner of, let's say, five or six bottles of wine. Over the course of a couple of weeks, give them a try. Now the homework part. Granted this is homework, but it's wine homework. . .isn't that fun? Anyway, as you try each of the wines, take a few notes, like "this one was too acid," "this one was too sweet," "this one had a good finish that I really liked," and "this one was like biting into my favorite fruit." You can visit the retailer, notes in hand, discuss what you liked or didn't like, and start the whole delicious process over again.

Saving Unfinished wine is as Simple as Saving Iced Tea

So you seriously think about opening a good, none-too-cheap bottle of wine for your own consumption. But you have second thoughts because you don't want the remaining half-bottle to turn bad and end up going down the drain.

Fear not, there are several ways to keep a good deal of a wine's flavor for several evenings. Here is a quick, easy and environmentally responsible way to do the trick.

Rather than jamming the cork back into the opened bottle, possibly cracking the cork, one of the best ways to save unfinished wine is to pour it into an emptied resealable, individual-sized iced tea or glass (never plastic) bottle like the ones Snapple, Taos Teas and Perrier come in.

Using the resealable glass bottle to store leftover wine is a variation on the screw-top wine bottle we talked about. Wine turns when it is exposed to air, and the screw top greatly decreases the wine's exposure to air.

If you don't have enough wine to fill the resealable glass bottle up to its neck, you should use a VacuVin. The VacuVin pump comes with rubber corks, or gaskets, that you insert in the mouth of a partially filled bottle. Then with the pump placed tightly over the top of the rubber cork, you rapidly pump the oxygen out of the bottle. The VacuVin pump is also a decent little workout for the old triceps. I can hear the infomercial British guy insisting, "Throwing leftover wine away is like cash in the trash. With the VacuVin you can save that leftover wine and get your arms toned at the same time. Soon you will be wearing your favorite sleeveless shirts with added confidence knowing that you look fabulous and not a single drop of wine was wasted!" The VacuVin, for what it saves you in leftover wine, is a real bargain at around $15.00. You can find it at most wine and housewares stores.

Back to the Wine Connection

You are now in the process of building your own wine connection; they may even start putting aside special things they think you might like. I'll bet that if all goes well, your relationship with the wine connection can become about as important, and as rewarding, as the other key personal service relationship you have—like the one with your hairdresser.

Can't Afford the Finest? Buy "Second Label" Wines.

Many of the world's great wine estates, famous for expensive wines, also produce what are called "second label" wines. While these wines may not be as earthshakingly great as a grand winery's top wines, they are usually very good, reflecting the qualities that make the winery's top-of-the-line wines what they are.

Say you get the chance to taste a super-expensive top-of-the line wine, and you love it. Go to your wine connection and find out what it costs. If it's beyond your budget, ask whether that winery produces a second wine. If it does, buy it and give it a try. You may be in for a real treat.

One way to look at this high/low wine scenario is by comparing it to fashion. Certainly there aren't many of us mortals who can afford couture from Marc Jacobs, Karl Lagerfeld, or Giorgio Armani, but we can buy their *prêt à porter* clothing at department stores. Second label garments are not as exclusive as couture ware, but they carry the same basic quality design points.

It boils down to good business. A quality fashion or wine house needs the second labels to support its higher-end, astronomically expensive goods. Cheval Blanc was made famous to those outside the wine world when, in the movie *Sideways*, Miles drinks this extraordinary wine while he eats a hamburger. Miles could have saved the Cheval Blanc for a more important occasion and eaten the burger with Cheval's much more affordable, and perfectly good, second label Le Petit Cheval.

Wine from Mouton Cadet that can be found in many grocery stores and wine shops, is another label to the historically significant and very expensive Chateau Mouton-Rothschild.

Believe me, there is no reason to hesitate to ask about second label wines: few of us can habitually drink wines that cost more that $50 a bottle.

Good examples of First & Second Label Wines

1st Chateau Lafite-Rothschild & 2nd Caruades de Lafite
1st Chateau Margaux & 2nd Pavillon Rouge de Margaux
1st Chalone Vineyards & 2nd Echelon
1st Stag's Leap Wine Cellars & 2nd Hawk's Crest
1st Duckhorn Vineyards & 2nd Decoy
1st Woodward Canyon Washington & 2nd Nelms Road
1st Tenuta dell'Ornellaia & 2nd Le Volte

Hesitant About the Wine Connection Idea?

You may not want to make an appointment with a wine professional because you don't want to be snubbed. What if they say, "Who are you, anyway? You're not a wine buyer for a restaurant." There is no reason to believe this will happen. First, the wine connection's *raison d'etre* is to sell wine. Second, wine people love to talk about wine, and will do it until they're blue in the face. Don't let this endless wine discussion be off-putting, as my colleagues in the wine trade mean well and enjoy their work. Wine pros will not be condescending towards you, but will make every effort to try to get you a wine you will truly like. They'll use the "help me help you" approach, to the satisfaction of both of you, and they'll be thrilled if, based on their good counsel, you buy even a single bottle of wine and better if you like it and return to shop again.

Chances are, you will learn oodles from a wine connection in a very short time.

Judging Wine by its Label

People often get confused and intimidated by wine labels, which can be very sketchy about what's inside a bottle. A vague label may say something like the wine goes well with fish, meat or pasta, but don't automatically dismiss a wine because the label is low on details. The thing is, the wine may actually be pretty good.

Then again, in many cases labels provide more detail than you'll ever need in a hundred years. I mean, unless you're a wine collector or a sommelier, why on earth should it really matter to you how much *titratable acidity* is left in the wine?

I'm no different from any consumer who can be attracted to buying a bottle of wine because of a clever name like *Wrongo Dongo, Screw Kappa Napa, Smoking Loon* or even *Cat's Pee on a Gooseberry Bush*. Interesting art on a label catches my attention too. As I have mentioned, Chateau Mouton-Rothschild is king when it comes to arty, cool labels. A good color palate on a label attracts my taste buds, too. I particularly like Veuve Clicquot's orange label; it always makes my mouth water for a glass of Champagne.

What I do tend to shy away from are wines with labels that are too ornate. That can include labels bearing anything from blinding decorative patterns to eye-straining family crests.

Heavy Bottles Mean There Are Great Things Inside

When I worked in a wine store, I was never excused from the job of lifting heavy wine cases; some weighed forty pounds or more. When I looked closely at the cases I had to lift, I noticed that some of the more "tony" wines, those priced at $100 or more per bottle, came in heavier bottles. This led me to think about the psychological aspects of purchasing wine. The heavy bottles of those expensive wines felt great in my hands: it was like holding an Oscar. It seemed to me that the contents in a heavy bottle must be really good because the producer had gone to the trouble of putting it in such a substantial container. I thought that winemakers must have put a ton of marketing thought into this.

So you're at a favorite wine shop, looking at thousands of bottles of wine, when one particularly handsome bottle catches your eye. You pick it up and notice immediately its heavy, solid feel. That sensation alone convinces you that it must be a quality wine of substance. Despite the high price tag you go ahead and splurge. See if you ever react this way.

From the Alpana Files: Bottle Shapes and What They Mean to You

Going up and down the aisles of your favorite wine retailer, you will notice that all manner of wines come in all manner of bottle shapes. Knowing the "bottle shape code" will help you understand what you're looking at, and find what you want in pretty quick order.

The Bordeaux bottle: Cabernet Sauvignon, Merlot, Sauvignon Blanc, Semillon and other varietals indigenous to the Bordeaux region, come in bottles with straight sides and tall shoulders, in dark green glass for the reds, lighter green glass for the dry whites and clear glass for the sweet whites.

The Burgundy bottle: Pinot Noir and Chardonnay-based wines are put into the more feminine-shaped Burgundy bottle with gently sloping shoulders and wider curves.

The Rhone bottle: Châteauneuf-du-Pape, Cotes du Rhone or Syrah/Shiraz will be put into bottles that are similar in style to the feminine Burgundy bottle, but not as wide. Wines from the Châteauneuf-du-Pape region will feature a raised coat of arms on the glass.

The Champagne bottle: In this, style meets function. Thick green glass, gently sloping shoulders and a dimple on the bottle's bottom (called a "punt") not only make the Champagne bottle look cool, but do a good job of preserving the precious fizz. These design features are necessary for the bottle to withstand the pressure (which, as I said, can be as much as a bus tire) created by effervescent Champagne. By the way, the rich and attractive dark green glass prevents harmful light from damaging the valuable liquid inside.

The German Flute bottle: The tall fluted German and Alsacienne bottles may conjure up thoughts of ghastly and sugary-sweet Blue Nun wine. The laws in Germany and Alsace mandate, with a couple of exceptions, that all wines in these regions be placed in flute bottles. The shape of the bottle should not lead you to believe that all these wines are sweet. In fact, most of the wine coming from Alsace is actually dry and tasty. In Germany, the color of the glass can tell you where the wine comes from: wines from the Mosel are packaged in green bottles, Rhine wines in brown bottles.

The Fortified Wine bottle: Fortified wines, such as Port, Madeira and Sherry, are put into smaller, squatter bottles with a wide shoulder. This design supposedly helps catch the sediment when these aged wines are decanted. Also, if the bottle is sealed with a longer-than-usual cork, it is meant to be aged. If the bottle has a shorter cork, this means the wine can be opened and enjoyed immediately.

Knowing What's Inside from Wine Label Details

Here are some helpful points to keep in mind so you can better understand what's going on inside the bottle simply by looking at the label.

- A body part, a saint, a geographical feature (even a body of water) on a label is a good indicator that the wine is from Australia. And there are animals. When you go shopping for Australian Shiraz you may find yourself falling for some very cagey marketing. This nice 'n' fruity wine often has graphics of animals on the label. Giraffes, monkeys, kangaroos, goats and many other members of the animal kingdom appear on the labels of this and many other types of Australian wine.

- European wines are named after the region they come from. They seldom indicate the variety of grape the wine is made from.

- American wines are named by the type of grape that the wine is made from.

- "Supérieur" on a label does not necessarily mean that the contents are superior or better. The French term "supérieur" and the Italian equivalent, "superiore" merely indicate that the wine has a slightly higher alcohol content.

- For American wines, only 75% of the named grape has to be in the wine. The remaining 25% doesn't have to be listed.

- If a wine is a blend, the winery may decide to list the specific grape varietal percentages on the back label. You'll probably be familiar with the many grape varieties used to create a blend. For instance, on an American, produced blend the label may read 55% Merlot, 25% Cabernet Sauvignon and 20% Syrah.

  On Australian wine labels, all the grape varieties used to make the wine must be listed in the order of their percentage of dominance.

- When you see the word "table wine" on an American wine label, it doesn't mean that it is just an "okay" or ordinary wine. The wine inside could actually be a real winner. American wines between 7% and 14% alcohol have only to be labeled simply as "table wine" without a specific alcohol percentage listed.

- Wine will be more full-bodied if the alcohol content on a label reads 14% or higher.

- Wine will be sweeter if the alcohol content on a label reads 9.5% or lower.

- "Riserva/Reserva" on a label of a European wine means that that particular wine was aged for a longer time in accordance with the laws of the region where it was produced. These wines usually cost a little more because the producer must manage the bottle longer. The additional aging of " Riserva/Reserva" wines helps mellow out the intense tannins found in these particular wines.

- "Reserve" on a label of U.S. or New World wines (the Western Hemisphere, including South America) can mean whatever producers want it to mean. There are no production mandates in the Americas as there are in Europe. In most cases, New World reserve wines cost more and have greater texture and richness than their non-reserve counterparts. Unfortunately, the term "reserve" does not always mean that the wine is better.

• Vintage (date displayed on the label) designates the year in which the grapes were harvested, not bottled. I'll take heat for this one. A wine's *vintage* only matters if the wine comes from a very specific appellation (precise, exacting location where the grapes for the wine are grown) and/or costs over $15 a bottle. Less expensive wines tend to be made from a blend of appellations that can sometimes be hundreds of miles apart. The vintage winemaker also goes to great lengths to keep the flavor consistent year after year so as not to disappoint their loyal followers.

• With a few exceptions, the simpler the wine label, the more expensive the wine.

Warning to All Wine Buyers!

Look out for U.S. wine labels that have a location name as part of the brand's name: for instance, if a winery has a name like Sonoma Cellars, that doesn't mean that the wine's fruit is from the Sonoma Valley. A pizzeria in Boise, Idaho, may be called New York Pizza, but that doesn't necessarily mean their pizza will taste like a New York pizza. You should double check the label to see from what appellation the wine originates. Legislation is pending to rein in this "iffy" wine practice.

Champagne Labels . . .
Wait a Sec! Demi is no Brut!

Across the labels of Champagne or sparkling wines you will see
the designations Brut, Extra-Dry and Demi-Sec. These words
are very important for you to understand even if you're buying
inexpensive wines. If you don't know them it could mean the
difference after a taste of wine between an "Ooo-eee!" and a
"Pittooo-eee!" When a Champagne or sparkling wine is being
bottled, the winemaker will often add additional sugar to the
wine in order to soften and balance out the acidity. The same
thing happens when you add sugar to lemonade: it balances out
and softens the lemon acidity. This process, called DOSAGE,
determines which of the following designations a bottle of
Champagne receives:

When the label says . . .

>   . . . ***Extra Brut:*** the wine has little to no sugar added
>   during the wine-making process; it is the driest
>   Champagne you will find.

>   . . . ***Brut:*** the wine is almost bone-dry. The designa-
>   tion "Brut" comes from the French word meaning
>   "crude" or "raw." This is also the most widely avail-
>   able style of Champagne.

>   . . . ***Extra-Dry:*** the wine is a touch sweeter than a Brut.
>   You'll find this designation only on the less reputable
>   sparkling wines like Korbel.

>   . . . ***Sec:*** the wine is actually twice as sweet as a Brut. For
>   no other reason than possibly to create confusion,
>   the word "Sec" is French for "dry."

... **Demi-Sec***: the wine is medium-dry. If you remember your high school Romance Language studies, you'll know that the prefix "Demi" means "Medium."

... **Doux***: the wine is very sweet.

* Wines with this designation are a little difficult to find, but if you are lucky enough to come across them, they go particularly well with desserts.

Champagne Labels . . . Part Deux

If the label on a bottle of Champagne says . . .

... **NV**: it means Non-Vintage. And while this may sound like this sparkler is No-Good, the NV distinction simply means the wine was made from a blend of different years. Blending allows winemakers greater flexibility in maintaining consistency in the flavor of a wine from one year to the next. So, whenever you order a bottle of NV Veuve Clicquot or NV Perrier Jouet, it will taste exactly like your last bottle of NV Veuve Clicquot or NV Perrier Jouet.

... **MV**: it means Multi-Vintage, which is just a nicer way of saying Non-Vintage.

... **Blanc de Blancs**: it means "white from white." Blanc de Blancs are white wines made from only white grapes, usually Chardonnay. The wine's acidity level therefore will be higher, giving the wine more of a green-apple tang.

. . . *Blanc de Noirs:* it means "white from red."
Blanc de Noirs are essentially white wines
made from red grapes. Since the color
of wine comes from grape skins, if you
remove the skins of these grapes from the
wine-making process immediately after
they have been crushed, the wine will
be white, rather than pink or red. The
flavor of Blanc de Noirs tends to be
earthy and fruity.

. . . *Rosé:* the wine's color will be pink.
This is the result of a limited amount
of skin contact in the wine-making process, or the wine is a blend
of white wine with a small amount of
red wine. Being pink does not mean
the wine is sweet or is a less sophisticated
wine. In the world of Champagne, Rosé is often the
rarest and most expensive style of Champagne available. Ironically, this wine, with what some may say
is a wimpy color, is the most full-bodied and robust
style of sparkling wine and is a perfect match with
juicy red meats and rich chocolates.

. . . *Cuvee:* it means the wine is a blend or mix.

From the Alpana Files:
Appellations . . . a Guide to
Good Wine Origin

When you don't recognize specific winery names, you should know the following famous appellations (wine regions), that produce the best wines using the corresponding grapes, to help you make the best wine selections.

United States

California

- Russian River—Pinot Noir & Zinfandel
- Green Valley, Sonoma—Sparkling Wine
- Knights Valley, Sonoma—Cabernet Sauvignon, Merlot
- Mendocino—Pinot Noir, Chardonnay, Gewürztraminer
- Rutherford, Napa Valley—Cabernet Sauvignon, Merlot
- Edna Valley—Chardonnay, Pinot Noir
- Sierra Foothills—Zinfandel, Sangiovese
- Howell Mountain, Napa Valley—Cabernet Sauvignon, Zinfandel
- Carneros—Chardonnay & Pinot Noir, Sparkling Wine
- Santa Maria Valley—Pinot Noir & Rhone Varietals
- Paso Robles—Zinfandel & Rhone Varietals
- Monterey—Chardonnay & Pinot Noir
- Dry Creek Valley—Zinfandel

Oregon

- Willamette Valley—Pinot Noir & Pinot Gris

Washington State

- Yakima Valley—Cabernet Sauvignon & Merlot
- Columbia Valley—Cabernet Sauvignon & Merlot
- Walla Walla—Cabernet Sauvignon & Merlot

International

Argentina

- Mendoza—Malbec, Bonarda and Torrontes

Australia

- Barossa Valley—Shiraz
- Clare Valley—Riesling
- McLaren Vale—Grenache and Shiraz
- Victoria—Pinot Noir
- Margaret River—Cabernet Sauvignon and Chardonnay
- Hunter Valley—Semillon
- Coonawarra—Cabernet Sauvignon and Merlot

Chile

- Maipo Valley—Merlot, Cabernet Sauvignon, Carmenere, Chardonnay
- Casablanca—Pinot Noir, Sauvignon Blanc, Chardonnay

New Zealand

- Marlborough District—Sauvignon Blanc.
- Hawkes Bay—Merlot and Cabernet Sauvignon
- Otago—Pinot Noir

Shopping for the Wine Bargain

Shopping for bargain wines can often be compared to the "last call" sales at a department store like Neiman Marcus. Of course they have a last call sale at Neiman Marcus for the practical reason that they need to make room for the next season's merchandise. This is often the case with bargain wines. A wine can become a bargain starting anywhere up or down the wine-selling chain. Producers, distributors and retailers, at some point, simply have to make room for new wines coming in.

For one reason or another, some perfectly okay wines just don't fly off the shelf the way *Two-Buck Chuck* did in '04. Thus there are plenty of good wines out there at cheap prices!

Wine Bargain "Whys?"

So why does merchandise go on sale? Most of us have become conditioned to believe that a garment is placed on sale because it may be torn, stained or have a pull, or just be missing a button. As with sale clothing, there are telltale signs that show why some wines end up in the bargain bin. Some of these signs we're about to describe may surprise you, as a sale wine can end up being both a bargain and perfectly enjoyable.

Beware of Brown

Say you're scrutinizing the selections at your wine retailer and you spot a familiar name on sale. If the wine comes in a translucent bottle, pick it up and hold it in front of a plain white surface—even your white sleeve will do—to see if the liquid is taking on a brownish color. If you think it's browning, show it to one of the floor pros. If everyone agrees that its brown, it's been there too long and should be avoided.

 *From the Alpana Files:*
Half-Bottles Don't Mean Half Price

A common misconception is that half-bottles of a wine are half the price of a full-sized 750ml (ml = milliliter) bottle of the same wine. In actuality, half-bottles cost more, to a pretty sizeable increase per ml, than a full-size bottle. To make half-bottles, wine producers need smaller labels, additional labor and special equipment, all of which add to the unit costs. For these reasons, many wineries don't even bother making half-bottles. Also, the wine in half-bottles ages faster than wine in standard 750ml. This, depending on the specific wine, can be a real plus or minus.

Bigger Bottles—Not Always Better

It works the same way with oversized bottles of wine, like magnums of Champagne. You don't get a markdown because you're buying a greater amount of wine. As with half-bottles, oversized bottles require special effort to handle and produce, so they end up being much more expensive per ml.

Wine in oversized bottles ages more slowly, because the greater amount of wine is exposed to less oxygen. Then again, if you want to save a wine for the long haul, it's not a bad idea to see if you can buy the wine in an oversized bottle.

Home Test

Let's say you examine a suspicious-looking, but interesting, wine on sale. I suggest you buy just one bottle. Take it home and if it tastes okay and it's a good deal, hurry back and buy an armful. But if the test bottle proves to be less then drinkable, it may have been shelved too long. You should return it and get a refund. Please don't buy into the myth that you can't return funny-tasting wine. Bad wine is as returnable as a container of milk that has soured.

Handling the Bottle

Another way to check a bargain wine is to run the tip of your finger very slowly under the bottle's neck foil to see if there's a tacky stickiness. If this is the case, the wine is leaking through and you need to alert the store and find a bottle without this defect. If you notice that a bottle's cork has bubbling near it, or seems to be pushed out, same deal; sound the alert.

One last warning sign that a wine may have gone bad is the level of wine in the bottle. If there seems to be wine missing, meaning the wine appears lower than the bottle's shoulder, it's likely to be a problem wine.

When in Doubt, Ask About the Wine

If you think for any reason a bargain wine you'd like to try looks risky, ask the retailer if they've had any other complaints about that particular wine. They may just open the bottle up right there for you to taste with them and check whether the contents are up to spec.

Shoes You Never Wear and Wine You Never Drink

How many of us have bought a pair of sale shoes, taken them home, realize we hate them and never wear them again? Well, there is a potential use for a bargain wine that turns out to be blah-city. You can at least cook with it. The shoes can go to Goodwill.

Say "No way!" to Old Chardonnay

If you're scanning the bargain shelves for white wines like Sauvignon Blanc, Pinot Grigio, Pinot Gris and Chardonnay, and you see any that are five or more years old, that is a reason they are on sale. Light wines this old just shouldn't be drunk; they aren't structured enough, like medium and heavy reds such as Zins, Shiraz, Bordeaux and Merlots, to withstand the test of time.

A Shot in the Dark . . . Buying from Wine Clubs

You know about the Book-of-the-Month and Fruit-of-the-Month clubs, but did you ever dream there could be a Bacon-of-the-Month club? Well, there is such a club and guess who joined it? I signed up, and paid in advance, because I really love bacon almost as much as I love wine, in all its glorious forms.

My passion for bacon probably stems from the fact that I was forbidden, for religious reasons, to eat it when I was a kid. As you know, if you forbid a child to do something, she'll obsess about it for the rest of her life. I won't even get into what a Catholic School education did to my brain.

So, what better way to satisfy my constant jones for bacon, without even having to get out of my pajamas to buy it? You should stay in your pajamas when you cook bacon. Makes it taste better, trust me.

In this program, every month I would receive a different artisinal bacon selection. Although it was fun to try designer bacons from across the country, I found that in the end, I really enjoyed only about 40% of the selections. It would have been much easier, and cheaper, for me just to head over to a specialty grocer and buy artisinal brands one at time instead of playing bacon roulette every month.

That was the last time I joined an Anything-of-the-Month Club. What I had discovered, from this and other experiences, is that these offers are based on either one person's taste or taste calculated to satisfy the broadest number of people.

Now after that, you won't be surprised by my advice about signing on with Wine-of-the-Month clubs. While it's fun to anticipate a new wine arriving every month, wine clubs can provide only a wine selection based on a broad theme such as Taste of Sonoma, Taste of Australia, Red Wines of the World, and so on. What the clubs don't very successfully supply is the specific information you need to choose a program that you may enjoy. As a result, wine clubs can never really match wines to your specific tastes. Essentially, you go on blind faith when you sign on with wine clubs.

I can comment on Wine-of-the-Month clubs from my own experience because early in my career, when I was with a wine retailer, we tried with great difficulty to pull together sweeping subscription programs people would like. Without having solid personal taste data, this was really, really tough for our team to do. We could only hope that the selection, based on our own tastes, would please many. Basically, there's a good chance that the wines from a wine club's broad general selection will not meet your expectations.

The Wine Club Gouge

You want to be sure that you are not overcharged by less scrupulous Wine-of-the-Month clubs for wines that are marketed and packaged under catchy titles like "Wines from Down Under, Mate!" Other questionable wine clubs practices include trying to unload overstocked items on unsuspecting and trusting wine lovers.

One Good Wine Out of Twelve Ain't Bad

Let's say you go ahead and join a wine club, despite my warning. If you do end up falling in love with, say, one out of a dozen eclectic choices, the problem then arises that you may never be able to find that winner again. You can contact the club administrators and ask, but in all likelihood the one out of twelve you really, really liked was from a limited selection. Unfortunately, you can pretty much expect to be discouraged if you go looking for the "one out of twelve" at a favorite wine store too. Chances are the retailers will tell you that the wine was a one-shot deal or one that their distributor doesn't have, or doesn't even know about.

Wine-of-the-Month clubs can help expand your wine knowledge by introducing you to new wine-producing regions. From my bacon experience, for instance, I discovered that the official bacon of the U.S. Olympic Team comes from New Hampshire. I certainly enjoyed it, but hard as I looked, I could never find it again. Nevertheless, since then I've always had an eye peeled for good New Hampshire bacons.

High-risk, Low-Reward Wine

I think that the Wine-of-the-Month path to wine enjoyment is, for the most part, an educational tool. Joining a club can be a good way to learn what wines and wine styles, you don't care for. Generally I think wine clubs are high-risk, low-reward investments. But there are notable exceptions.

Like Having Your Own Personal Master Sommelier

One exception is the very fine Ferry Plaza Wine Merchant in San Francisco. I can personally vouch for these folks because one of the managing partners is Peter Granoff, a terrific Master Sommelier. Peter got his MS on the first try, It took me three trips to the Court of Master Sommeliers to do it. Peter goes to great lengths to select only the best wines for the club, and he shares my distaste for unscrupulous merchants who use wine clubs as a way to dump their overstocks.

Ferry Plaza Wine Merchant offers extremely well-priced wines from many regions. Peter has even been known to place a phenomenal $10 bottle in with a subscription mix from time to time. Go take a look for yourself at www.fpwm.com

Wines Bought at Auction . . . Charity Functions

Good Cause events can provide you the opportunity to buy great wine at silent auction for bargain prices and receive a tax deduction up to the market value of the wine. Never a bad thing.

Whether the cause is for the arts, good works, politics, health care or education, these charities are often high-profile and call upon people with excellent access to private collections of wine to make donations. There's a possibility that many attending these affairs may not know much about wine, so with your wide-ranging knowledge of wine, gleaned from *Alpana Pours*, you could, to use a metaphor, have a shot at acquiring a flawless diamond at *Diamonique* prices.

As with for-profit wine auctions, there are usually pre-tastings days before wine auction charity events. This will give you a chance to sample the goods and plan your strategy to buy low. Good luck!

Wines Bought at Auction . . . Profit & Loss at For-Profit Functions

A quick word about for-profit wine auctions. Once you go online to find wine auctions, you may want to visit an auction site to take advantage of the pre-tasting of the difficult-to-find wines these events usually feature. While you will pay something for this pre-auction privilege, glass for glass it's much less expensive then buying a bottle of rare wine at a straight retail price.

As with any auction, go into bidding with your homework done and a budget in mind. While you may sense some really good deals, do yourself a favor and find out what the market value is before the auction day.

Auctions are great places to find older and rarer wines. The trick is to make sure that the wines are in good condition. Start by checking the fill on wines of interest to make sure they are not lower than the base of the bottle's neck. In most cases, the auction house won't tell you from whom they purchased the wines, but they should tell you about the wines' recent storage conditions. If you discover a wine has been moved around a lot, take a pass on it.

Final For-Profit Wine Auction Warning

Wine bidders beware, because sometimes for-profit auctions can be ego-driven affairs. The cost of a case of wine can rise, not because it is rare or special, but because the bidder wants to save face, or impress others. If you can risk the possibility of turning a large fortune into a small one, or love a challenge, for-profit wine auctions may be for you.

Win-e People Over

AT PARTIES, SHOWERS, WEDDINGS, ANNIVERSARIES . . . AND WITH WINE GIFT GIVING

Wine and Party Time

You may be surprised to know that the services of a sommelier aren't limited to making wine recommendations to small
groups of diners. At Everest, I was often deeply involved with
people choosing wine for large functions and events with
anywhere from ten to as many as 300 guests. I have been called
upon to make recommendations for elaborate weddings, corporate dinners, 80th birthdays, holiday parties and, once, even
a divorce celebration. It can indeed be a stressful experience
trying to select wines for a party along with the menu, linens,
flowers, music and exotic male dancer, if that's the type of bash
you are throwing. Part of my job therefore was to calm nervous
event hosts and assure them that everything was going to be
just wine fine. Most of these hosts had the same questions for

me. How much wine will be needed? Will the wine pair well with the food? How should the wine be served? And the most important question of all, always: how much will the wine cost?

If you are in the midst of planning a party with a wine focus, read on, since all these questions have practical answers.

From the Alpana Files:
The Quick-Turn Wine Party Plan

Recently, I read that more and more 20-somethings like to throw informal parties. Even though it may be a quickie, you should still have a plan to control cash outlay and the stress on your brain cells and stomach lining.

Here are some quick 'n' easy ways to pull together your wine festival for friends.

- *Ask yourself what kind of party you'd like to throw.* Think about a theme, the size and the mood of the party you'd like to create. Maybe a Spanish tapas-style fete for six, or pre-made hors d'ouevres for forty? If you like to cook, a sit-down meal may be for you. Making these basic decisions will help guide your wine selection. Whatever you decide, make sure you devise a plan that allows you to join in the fun and not get stuck in the kitchen.

- *Serve food-friendly wines.* Wines that pair well with a variety of foods include Sauvignon Blanc, Pinot Noir, Zinfandel, Sangiovese, Merlot and sparkling wine—all safe crowd-pleasers.

- *Wine serves itself.* Having wine as the beverage of choice at your party allows guests to serve themselves, at, say, a wine buffet. Self-serve wine also saves you from having to create elaborate mixed drink set-ups all evening long.

- *Estimating at five glasses of wine per bottle, make a "wine buy" plan based on two glasses per guest.*

- *Don't wait for a special occasion, have Champagne!* Champagne can be enjoyed with any part of a meal, or for any reason. Delicious and affordable sparkling wines like Spanish Cava or Italian Prosecco are great substitutes for the real thing.

- *You can drink wine out of anything.* To create a casual party atmosphere, buy festive plastic tumblers or goblets. You can find nice ones almost anywhere you buy party goods. If you really need stemware, discount stores often stock basic stemware for $1.25 a glass or less.

- *Leftovers, even wine, are one of the best things about having a party.* If you're lucky enough to have opened bottles of wine left after a party, re-cork the wine and refrigerate it. Then you can relive your party for days to come!

- *Wine doesn't need to be expensive to be fun and delicious.* There are good $10 (and below) bottles or wine galore. Before the get-together, pick up some inexpensive wines you think your guests may enjoy. After trying them out, head back to the store and stock up on the ones you'd like to serve at your shindig.

The SRO Party

When it comes to picking wines for parties where guests are standing or milling about, my advice is *keep it simple*. "Simple" meaning that the number of wine selections you offer should be limited (not the quantity of wine—just the choices—we don't want a riot). And don't think you need to sacrifice flavor in order to keep the budget in line. There are plenty of tasty, modestly priced wines out there. Besides, throwing impressive, expensive wines at people at a casual party is like wasting the debut of a pair of really hot, pricey shoes at the ballpark where no one pays any attention to your feet. As a matter of fact, unless you're planning a more formal party requiring a major "wow moment," you should consider the many decent and very palatable sale wines that are frequently available at respectable wine stores. However, don't purchase budget brand wines found on every grocery store shelf in America. You don't want to inadvertently clue your guests in on how much, or how little, you spent on the wine.

The ten people or more rule

When it comes to parties with ten or more guests, you may want to limit the wine offerings to one white and one red. This way you avoid confusing party guests with too many wine choices or the need to change glasses. This will also keep you or any servers you may have, from being forced to keep track of more than two wines and who chose what.

I advocate serving modestly priced wines for SRO style gatherings because guests at these functions tend to focus their attention on socializing or schmoozing and aren't paying much attention to what they may be drinking. Enjoying wine at these kinds of parties becomes not so much a reason for the gather-

WIN-E PEOPLE OVER   143

ing, as a social lubricant. I'm not saying that you should serve jug wines, but you probably should save that case of super-expensive couture wine for other occasions, when your guests can focus on the wine.

A savvy approach to making a good party wine statement is to serve obscure selections retailing at $15 or less per bottle rather than the usual predictable Chardonnay and Shiraz. Head to your wine shop and ask for quality, inexpensive wines from the lesser-known varietals of Italy, Portugal, Argentina and, especially, Spain. Just think how impressed your guests will be when they taste your "international wine selection." I can hear a guest now, saying, "Hey, this wine is really tasty, what is it?" This will give you the opening to respond, "Oh, its a little number from a winery in Valencia off the coast of Southern Spain. Glad you like it." *Bargain wine + international caché = guests way impressed and host not broke.*

How much wine will you need?

Have you ever been to a party where the host runs out of wine? Not much fun. Given this potential disaster scenario, it is always better to purchase too much wine than not enough. Even if wine is not the only beverage on hand, people tend to stay with the drink they begin a party with. If it was wine and there isn't any more, you're sunk.

So then, exactly how much wine do you buy? A nifty formula for determining this is to multiply the number of guests by .75 (3/4 of a bottle). Using that formula, for fifteen guests you would need almost twelve bottles, or a full case. Purchasing a full case may earn you an additional discount of 5-10% at many wine shop checkouts. While this may seem like a lot of wine, when guests are standing they tend to consume more wine than when they're sitting down. This is because wineglasses at SROs are, in guests' hands, in constant use.

Unfortunately, there is no rule of thumb when it comes to purchasing more white or red wine. Personally, I tend to stick to white wines at parties because I find they go better with socializing and also because I rarely graze. Whites are also much easier to clean when I spill some on myself.

Have plenty of glasses

By going with the two-wine choice for the ten-or-more affair, you will need a good number of glasses. To figure out exactly how many, simply multiply the number of guests by 1.5 glasses. If you expect fifteen guests, you will need nearly two dozen glasses. It's a good idea to assume that over the course of the party every guest will try both the terrific red and wonderful white being served. However, there may be a guest or two who doesn't realize that it's perfectly acceptable to drink both wines from the same kind of glass. The .5 part of the wine glass equation helps you cover for the multiple-glass-using individuals.

Since not many of us have two dozen or more 6-ounce wine glasses (the best size for parties), you may want to look online or in the yellow pages for places that rent glassware. You can also go to Target, World Market, Crate & Barrel, Costco, wherever, and buy $1.99 wineglasses that you don't have to worry about. Funky colored beverage goblets can also be used. But unless you are throwing a beach party or very casual backyard BBQ, offering guests plastic wineglasses is sort of tacky.

From the Alpana Files:
Wine Glasses and ID Bracelets

Here's a fun way to help guests at a party keep track of their wineglasses. Find a chotchke shop that sells inexpensive toe rings. You can purchase toe rings in a myriad of colors and styles. As the guests arrive, ask each one to choose one. Show your guests how to wrap the toe rings, which are expandable, around the stem of their wineglasses. From that moment on, they will be able to identify which wineglass is theirs.

Wine for the "Sit Down" Dinner Party

Say you've caught the cooking bug and want to show off your kitchen skills by throwing a dinner party. You could spend hours poring over cookbooks, culinary websites and magazines to plan your elaborate menu, or you could do as a girlfriend of mine once did—call a caterer and pretend you cooked the meal yourself. Either way, the decision still must be made on what wine to serve at the "sit down."

First Impressions

A good host will always have a libation ready to serve guests as they arrive. This *greeting with wine* sets a very positive tone for the evening, no matter what happens later. Chilled sparklers like Prosecco (Italy), Cava (Spain) or Champagne (France) are great for greeting.

Still wines can also be served when guests arrive. You could serve the wines that you have chosen for the actual dinner, but I recommend you go with different wines for the apéritif. For this, choose selections from the light white and light red categories. The high acidity in the lighter wines stimulates the appetite. Serving lighter wines also allows more food pairing flexibility if you are serving a nice variety of hors d'oeuvres.

Later I'll discuss some wine-based cocktails, like Kirs, Kir Royales and Sangria, that can also be served as apéritifs certain to help the fun and festivity. Dry Sherries make a good pre-meal drink too.

However, for the nice "sit down," strong cocktails like Martinis or Margaritas, while good at kicking up the party noise level, don't do a lot to get guests to focus on the great wines and food you have prepared.

Wines for any "Sit Down" Menu

If you're planning a Continental or traditional sit-down dinner party, you can rely on most of my food-wine recommendations, which involve familiar foods and wines. But let's say you're planning to offer your guests something a little different. What do you do? Here are a couple of suggestions:

The Ethnic Dinner Party

If you plan your "sit down" around a favorite ethnic or ethnic regional cuisine, the best advice I can give you is to serve wines of the same region. This approach should present few problems, since almost every wine-producing country and region of the world makes at least one good, significant wine, and your guests will appreciate the complete ethnic food and wine spectrum. If all the ethnic food and wine meld well together, your sit down will be like taking your guests on a brief trip to a foreign country.

From the Alpana Files:
Food/Wine Pairings for
Ethnic Party Menus

While the following list hardly covers all the ethnic foods you could pair with wine, it gives you some insight into how certain ethnic and global cuisines and wines can work in harmony. After you look this over you will probably tend to experiment with your own ideas for pairing ethnic foods and wine. In each example the first wine is a white and the second a red.

- *Paella Fiesta (Spain)*—Albarino & Spanish Grenache
- *Roast Lamb (Greece)*—Moscophilero & Agioritiko
- *Bouillabaisse (France)*—White Bordeaux & Provencal Rosé
- *Fondues (Switzerland)*—Swiss Chasselas & Gamay
- *Shrimp on the Barbie (Australia)*—Australian Semillon & Shiraz
- *Osso Bucco (Italy)*—Soave & Amarone della Valpolicella
- *Classic BBQ (U. S.)*—Sauvignon Blanc & Zinfandel

While the following countries produce wines, they can be tricky to find. For tasty alternatives to regional wines, try the Western wines listed here.

- *Japan*—Gruner Veltliner & Pinot Noir
- *China (Hunan/Szechwan)*—Riesling & Cotes du Rhone
- *India*—Vouvray & Beaujolais

The Eclectic Dish Dinner Party . . . a.k.a. Pot Luck

If your menu is an eclectic global array of dishes (a.k.a. in the Singh household as "Potluck"), having available a wide range of different wines, from light whites to heavy reds, is a great way to go. For a Potluck, I often keep an assortment of open bottles of wine near, but not on, the dining table. It's a kind of wine station that allows everyone to break from the main table and choose wines they're interested in. It's also a fun way for everyone to taste a nice variety of wines.

At Parties Say Cheese! . . . and Wine too!

I've noticed that the comfort foods most popular with women usually have a common ingredient – cheese, glorious cheese! Whether it's a humble grilled cheese sandwich or a fancy wheel of French Brie, we women apparently can't get enough of it! So, let's look at both myth and fact about wine and its famous relationship with cheese

Growing up in an Indian household, I didn't know much about cheese except that it was yellow and slices of it came individually wrapped in plastic. It wasn't until I took a trip to Europe in my early twenties that I discovered how many different types of cheese there are in the world. Considering that almost every country produces some form of cheese (I eventually discovered that India makes a cheese called *paneer*) it would be nearly impossible to make a list of every single cheese available and the best wine to go with it.

Pairing wine with cheese may seem fairly complicated, but if you follow some simple guidelines, it's fun and easy. I pair high-acid cheese with high-acid wines, soft and creamy cheese with more full-bodied buttery whites or tart sparkling wines, hard cheese with firm-bodied reds, and I find that sweet wines work best with a wide range of cheeses, especially the more pungent ones.

From the Alpana Files:
Whom does Alpana go to for
Food & Wine Pairings?

Since I really enjoy cooking and entertaining, I can spend hours planning meals, and I frequently go online to look for recipes. During those searches I discovered that many websites, such as www.epicurious.com, also give pretty good food/wine pairing suggestions. While you may not always be able to find the exact recommendation, knowing the recommended wines will help your trusty wine shop to locate a good alternative for you.

Red Wine Not Always a Friend to Cheese

I will say that the common belief that all cheese should be paired with red wine is not entirely true. I have been saying for years that red wine and cheese do not, in many cases, make a good marriage. The reason is that the milk ingredient of cheese and the tannins in wine can blank each other out to the point that you can't quite fully taste either the cheese or the wine.

But don't despair, my wine-and cheese-loving friend. White wine, in its many incarnations, is usually a real winner with a great number of cheeses. I suggest you experiment to find out which wine and cheese pairings you like.

Here, then, are popular cheeses paired with both red and white wine selections.

CHEESE	WHITE	RED
Chèvre (from goat's milk, high acid and fresh)	Sancerre	Pinot Noir
Tallegio (from cow's milk, soft, creamy & pungent)	Alsace Pinot Gris	Nebbiolo
Morbier (from cow's milk, creamy, nutty & fruity)	Australian Semillon	Gamay
Manchego (from sheep's milk, hard & nutty)	Dry Fino Sherry	Rioja
Blue d'Auvergne a.k.a. Blue Cheese (from cow's milk, tart & creamy)	Sauternes	Port
Camembert (from cow's milk, soft & creamy)	Chardonnay	Cabernet Franc
Brie (from cow's milk, soft & buttery)	Champagne	Sangiovese
Cheddar (from cow's milk, firm, sharp & nutty)	Riesling	Shiraz

CHEESE	WHITE	RED
Mozzarella (from cow's milk, fresh & mild)	Pinot Grigio	Zinfandel
Gouda (from cow's milk, hard, caramel-like & nutty)	Viognier	Cabernet Sauvignon
Gruyere/Swiss (from cow's milk, firm & mushroom like)	Chenin Blanc	Syrah
Parmesan (from cow's milk, hard, toasty & savory)	Cava or Prosecco	Brunello
Havarti (from cow's milk, soft and subtle)	Sauvignon Blanc	Rioja
Spicy Monterey (My home town!) Jack (from cow's milk, soft, nut & zesty flavors)	Vouvray	Zinfandel

From the Alpana Files:
Cheese After the Entrée Means
More Wine Time

The French chef at an upscale restaurant where I once worked, was perplexed when Americans ordered cheese as an appetizer course. He said that Europeans ate cheese after the entrée because the enzymes (*Lactobacillus Bulgaricus* is the scientific name) in cheese help digestion. He said too that it was improper to eat a stinky plate of cheese if someone else at the table is having dessert, because the pungent aroma of cheese makes it difficult for the other diners to enjoy their flourless chocolate cake or tiramisu.

Another reason why it is better to enjoy cheese after the entrée, is that it is an excellent way to finish off whatever wine is left.

Wine for Showers, Weddings, Anniversaries, et al.

Now let's examine some wine and menu arrangements for important occasions: bridal and wedding parties, baby showers, bachelorette bashes, christenings and other festive occasions. We'll look into how to select and purchase the right amount, and successfully manage wine whether the event is in your home, at an hotel or in a restaurant.

Wine and the Bridal Shower

We will assume you are giving a shower and that the information here applies to either the "surprise" or "non-surprise" events. While I don't know the specific statistical breakdown, these fun affairs can take place in your digs or at a restaurant or hotel banquet room. If it's going to be at a restaurant or hotel, you should work out the wine and cocktails details with the venue staff. Have them go over possible wine ideas with you in advance. You don't want any surprises on the shower day—like the wine you chose is suddenly not available and you'll pay the same price for an inferior substitute. Also, get the "*What ifs*" questions out of the way. For instance, "*What if* someone is not having wine, will she be able to have a cocktail instead?" or "*What if* a guest doesn't like the wine selection?" I was frequently asked the second "What if" at Everest, and I would say the best response to the guest would be, "The wine we're having was selected by your host. May I offer you an iced tea or soft drink instead?" Make certain your venue has a similar "reaction plan."

Be firm when it comes to beverage details and potential crisis control. Otherwise, the venue may cave in to unauthorized guest requests, as when someone goes overboard and orders a $200 bottle of Champagne and has it put on your shower tab. Most important, clearly let the venue know what you want to spend and what beverages you will permit your guests to order.

When You Shower, You Have Bubbles

Most showers tend to be brunches, luncheons or teas. Look at what may be eaten at the typical shower; eggs Benedict, quiches, salads from chicken to Caesar to Niçoise, tea sandwiches, cookies, cakes, petit fours and other lighter pastries. With that kind of broad potential menu the last thing you want to do is plop a big, heavy wine, white or red, in front of guests. You want to select wines that, like the food, are light and delicate. Slam-dunk wines that easily meet shower criteria are Champagnes or wines that sparkle.

Sparkling wine, Champagne or otherwise, is also excellent for shower cocktails, especially those, like Bellinis and Mimosas, that are a nice mix of sweet and savory flavors of brunchy foods like eggs Benedict, French toast, quiche with bacon, Danish pastries and muffins.

You can use the same sparkling wine you plan to serve on its own in Bellinis (peach juice and sparkling wine, a.k.a. sparkler), Kir Royal (Crème de Cassis and a sparkler) Champagne cocktails (Cognac, Bitters, a sugar cube, lemon twist and a sparkler) and Mimosas (OJ and a sparkler). If budget is an issue, and you want to serve Bellinis and Mimosas, keep in mind that some restaurants charge just as much for a Bellini or Mimosa as for a full glass of Champagne. To find out, just ask.

Whenever someone asks me about the best Champagne to use in cocktails or punch I always say, "Use the best, least expensive one you can find." The reason: the moment you use Champagne as an ingredient for a cocktail or punch, the flavor of the wine competes with all the other fruity ingredients. And, after all, in a cocktail or punch, all you really want is the essence of the sparkler and the creamy mouth texture that tiny bubbles deliver.

Sparkling Wines are the New Champagne

While Champagne is always my first choice for any celebration, you can also have a great time enjoying Champagne-style sparkling wines like Franciacorta. Franciacorta is produced in one of Italy's newest high-quality sparkling wine-making regions. Look for the *Bella Vista* and *Ca' del Bosco* labels.

Prosecco is a wonderful fruity sparkler made with Prosecco grapes grown near the Veneto region of Italy. Prosecco is great to sip by itself or as the alcohol base of a fruit juice cocktail. Don't hesitate to try the *Nino Franco, Bisol* or *Mionetto* labels.

Many French wine-producing houses have set up camp in the Napa, Sonoma and Mendocino regions of California where they are now producing great California Sparkling Wines. Additionally, there are a handful of notable local producers, the best of which include *Roederer, Ironhorse, Domaine Carneros, Mumm Napa, Piper Sonoma, Domaine Chandon* and *Schramsberg*. These California sparklers tend to be a touch more fruit-forward than their French counterparts.

It may surprise you to learn that New Mexico is producing wonderful Champagne alternatives. It started when a couple of French guys were looking to invest in a Napa Valley sparkling winery. When they found the land was too expensive, they set up shop in fertile and reasonably priced New Mexico. Their sparkling wine, known as *Gruet*, can be purchased at around $15 a bottle, and would be a bargain at twice the price.

In Spanish, Cava means *cellar*. It is also a sparkling wine style produced from grape varieties grown in Spain in the area surrounding Barcelona. Two examples of Cavas you may have encountered include *Freixenet* (known by many for its distinctive black bottle with gold lettering) and *Cordorníu*. The Cava sparkling wine tends to be rather rustic and fruity. And while it may not have the finesse of Champagne, at Cava's competitive price, who can complain? If you want to try a couple of nice ones, look for *Segura Viudas* and *Montsarra*.

Sparkling wines that are produced within France but outside the Champagne region, are referred to as Cremant. Regions such as Bordeaux or Burgundy offer pretty decent Cremants, but my favorite is *Cremant d'Alsace*. The best of these are made with Pinot Blanc and Pinot Noir. Solid Cremant labels to try are *Lorentz, Lucien Albrecht, Pierre Sparr* and *Domaine Klipfel*.

France's famous Loire Valley offers a wide array of sparkling wines, from honey-kissed whites to fruity, dry and robust Rosés. Look for sparkling versions of *Vouvray, Montluis, Anjou* and *Saumur*. You may want to double-check with your retailer the sweetness level of these wines, which can vary, If you see the term "Mousseaux" on a Loire label it means it is a sparkling wine. If a Loire label says "Petillant," the wine inside is only slightly sparkling.

Most Australian wine-producing regions are too hot to produce delicate sparkling wines; fortunately there are a few cooler areas, in Victoria and on Tasmania, that turn out some well-priced sparkling wine. For a decent Aussie sparkler, look into *Seppelt, Seaview, Clover Hill* and Tasmanian *Domaine Chandon.*

Sparkler methods

Lastly, when you go shopping for specifically sparkling wines, ask the retailer if a sparkler you may be interested in was made using the *Champagne methode* or the *tank* (a.k.a. *charmat*) method. If your choice was made by the tank/charmat method it will have a grapey flavor; a selection made by the Champagne Methode will have a toasty flavor.

Chardon-no, Red-okay

For as early in the day as most bridal showers occur, a Chardonnay's butteriness will dominate most shower food flavors and have a mouthy feel that may not be very pleasing.

However, there are four reds that can be a delightful addition to the festivities: Pinot Noir, Gamay, Beaujolais and Sangiovese can brighten up the special daytime event with their lush colors, light feel and low tannin touch.

Even if you are serving reds, you can bring out a sparkler to toast the bride-to-be with something to go with the sweets

treats, like a Moscato d'Asti, or, if the dessert is serious chocolate, a Rosé sparkling wine that you have chosen for its luscious
raspberry flavor.

A "No-Pop!" Shower

If you do choose to serve light, non-sparkling (a.k.a. "still")
white wines with a bridal shower meal, I suggest you go with
Sauvignon Blanc, Vouvray or Pinot Grigio. These wines will
be well received because they can accommodate brunch foods,
which tend to have intermingled sweet and savory flavors, like
the aforementioned French toast, Danish pastries, eggs Benedict and buttery croissants. Wines like these nice whites offering a touch of sweetness and fruitiness, are the way to go.

Red wines are also a nice possibility for a shower beverage,
provided they too have a lighter profile. Reds like Pinot Noir,
Gamay or even a dry Rosé match extremely well with bacon,
ham or even roast beef.

Lunch and High Tea Wines

When the shower is a light lunch event, stick with a lighter white
that has higher acidity and a crisp texture, like Pinot Grigio,
Sauvignon Blanc or Dry Riesling. These wines work extremely
well when served with crunchy main-course salads and luncheon
sandwiches. Light reds like Pinot Noir and Gamay also work well.

If the shower is more of a high tea (mid-to-late afternoon)
affair, with tea sandwiches, nuts, cheeses, light pastry and cru-
dités, usually a basic sparkling wine will be very tasty and very
appropriate.

The Shower Calculation—How Much Wine Will I need?

With the likely exception that one bridesmaid will be drowning
her sorrows as she thinks something like, "When's it gonna be

my turn?"—most bridal shower attendees don't booze it up very much. If you intend to serve Champagne or sparkling wine, go with about half of a 750ml bottle per guest. If still wines make up your *carte du vin*, about half of a 750ml bottle should successfully serve your guests. Remember, if you're having the shower at your place, whatever you don't drink won't go bad. Let the wine "leftovers" be a little thank-you to yourself for throwing the party.

Wine and the Bachelorette Party

The Bachelorette party is a totally different animal from the bridal shower . . . and I do mean animal!

Since you are the *Maid* or *Matron of Honor*, you have to plan the surprise timing, choose and secure the party location, hire the male dancer and rent the stretch limo. My, you have an awful lot to do! Well, you have one more thing to do: stock the limo with WINE, and lots of it. This is, after all, the bride-to-be's last night of wild freedom. And you are responsible for making the event fun, memorable and somewhat stylish. *Note: Each vehicle requires a designated driver.*

All-Wine, All-the-Time

Before we go any further I have an adage for your review and consideration.

> *Liquor before wine, you're doing fine.*
> *Wine then liquor, you've never been sicker.*

The reason for sharing this nugget of wisdom with you is simple; if you can swing it, have an all-wine bachelorette party. That way, you can still have plenty of fun while preventing nasty hangovers from mixing wine and heavily boozed-up cocktails. This *ounce of prevention* also keeps away puffy *wedding-day-face* and general bloating.

So, if you're going for an all-wine-all-the-time party, you should probably start the evening with a Champagne or sparkling wine. While I drink Champagne for any number of lame reasons, to many people it is the traditional celebratory beverage. Sparklers also allow guests gradually, not expeditiously, to get into the spirit of what is usually the most raucous social drinking most will ever enjoy.

From the Alpana Files: Check your Bags

If you do overindulge at the bachelorette party and end up with an extra set of luggage under your eyes, I have a secret model's trick I learned from a makeup artist. Apply Preparation H under your eyes and watch the bags shrink. You'll still have a hangover that feels like a jackhammer is drilling through your brain, but at least you'll look fabulous.

Wild Reds for the Wild Night

As I cautioned earlier, it's probably a good idea if you have an *All-Wine, All-the-Time* bachelorette party. So far we've covered just about any wine with a bubble in it—now we need to mention some great *still* wines for this girl's ultimate night out. Here are some wild and sexy reds: Syrah, Red Burgundy, Amarone della Valpolicella, Grenache and Zinfandel.

Wine and The Big Day!

Champagne Wedding Dreams

As I mentioned earlier, while writing this book I've been in the throes of planning my own wedding. Naturally, like many of the people I've had the pleasure of helping with their weddings, I would love to have Champagne flowing from a fountain at my Big Day event. However, I live in the real world; I'm on a budget. Fortunately, when it comes to weddings, I know how to beat "hidden costs," get the best wine deals, order the right quantities of wine and what-not.

And yes, while brides are nervous and even panicked about every detail of their Big Day, when it comes to wine selection, they can easily take control, and actually have a lot of fun, just by following *Event Planner Singh's Tips on Wine for Weddings*.

Speaking of value and thrift, I have this handbag that everyone, man and woman, admires. You'd die of shock if I told you how little it cost. You want to find wedding wines that are like my inexpensive but attractive bag. The wines that taste high-priced, but are actually a steal.

From the Alpana Files:
A Tale of a Wedding Wine Disaster

I have this friend who told me about a nightmare wedding reception involving wine. This story should be a good lesson for everyone.

My friend and his wife were at a friend's fourth wedding; that was ominous in itself. At the appointed time, the hotel servers hurried around the table, offering a red or white to each guest. Meanwhile, in the clear view of everyone present, "Head Table 8," as my friends later contemptuously referred to the wedding party, were enjoying a continuous flow of the groom's favorite Champagne, Dom Pérignon.

Over the appetizer and salad courses all the wineglasses at my friend's table were emptied. Since my friend was a close pal of the groom's, he was chosen by his tablemates to tell the servers that everyone would like more wine. After talking with the Service Captain, my friend came back to the table with bad news: there was going to be only one glass of wine per person.

To add insult to injury, when it came time to toast the bride and groom, an inexpensive sparkling Chardonnay was served to all the guests while highly visible magnums of Dom Pérignon were still being poured for Head Table 8.

The result of these three wine-related *faux pas* was that for the rest of the affair, all the guests, except of course for those at Head Table 8, forgot to be thrilled about how beautiful the bride looked, how elegantly splendid the reception venue was, how tasty the food had been, how much fun the dancing was or how nice it was to see Aunt Ellen looking so well. The only thing all the guests at this wedding disaster will remember is not getting that second glass of wine, while Head Table 8 proceeded to get hammered on an artesian well of Dom.

The moral of this story is that unless you want to really tick off your wedding guests, the place to scale back on a huge costly affair is the food. Have chicken instead of beef, but never, ever cut back on the flow of liquor and wine.

Rule #1 for Selecting Wines for Weddings

Before we go any further, there is one immutable rule I implore
you to follow when selecting wines for the big day. Whatever
you choose for your reception, make certain that you taste it
before the Big Day.

As a matter of fact, you could have a party with members of
your bridal shower for the purpose of selecting wines for your
wedding. Why not have a bridesmaids' wine-tasting party? You
can also stage a tasting with only you and your man or your
parents. In preparation for this, ask the retailer, or the event
venue folks supplying the wine, to prepare a blind flight-style
tasting for you and yours. One thing, it is important not to
select the wines too far in advance, because the vintage may
change or there may not be enough supply available at the time
of the wedding. So do one of these fun wine-selecting sessions
no more than four-to-six weeks in advance of your Big Day.

Wines as Unique as You

Ask yourself, "Do I want people saying I saved a buck or two on
wine that can be seen in every grocery store's bargain bin? Or
do I want people saying, 'Wow, what a unique wine. Who knew
that corner of the world produced such great tasting wine!'?"
When it comes to a wedding, you want "unique" everywhere
you can get it, right? Well, a good, unique wine will get your
guests buzzing and taking home a fond wine memory to boot.

"Couture Wine" Availability Problems

Let's say he proposes to you under a beautiful oak tree in Napa
Valley. He whispered the words you'd been waiting ages to hear
and he does so as he pours a glass of one of the finest wines
around, say *Screaming Eagle Cabernet Sauvignon*. Let's also say
that you can afford to serve, for sentimental reasons, Scream-

ing Eagle Cabernet Sauvignon at your wedding reception. Let's say I'm the person handling the wine at the reception and you say the only wine you want at the reception is Screaming Eagle Cabernet Sauvignon. Then I say, that's a fine, rare and expensive wine—or as some like to call them a *Couture Wine*—and the available quantities are very limited and there's little hope of my establishment, or any other for that matter, being able to fulfill your dream wine request. Let's say you tear up and cry, "It's my day and I want it to be perfect!" I think to myself, "Get a grip, woman."

This is a frequent scenario when people have their hearts set on particular wines produced in small quantities. Even event venues have a hard time getting hold of small-volume Couture Wines. Let's just say it's a good idea to have a Plan B wine.

Rule #2 for Selecting Wines for Weddings

The other, slightly less immutable, rule is, try not to choose wines that are easily recognizable by name and price. Tell your event professional that you are willing to consider wines that have less recognizable names but are good-tasting. Consider wines from Argentina, South Africa, Spain, Italy or New Zealand that are all good and even unique. This will make your wine selection and your event even more memorable.

Wine Design That Says Who You Are

You can also select wines that reflect your personality. Visit a well-stocked wine retailer and look for clever label designs that express who you are and your sense of humor. There are wines with fine art, modern art, birds in flight, sea creatures, lovely hearts and even Roy Lichtenstein-style cartoons as part of their label design. If you're a "dog person" and everyone you care about knows that, *Chateau du Paws* is possibly the wine for your wedding. These unique label designs could help support your wedding theme and express what you and your groom are all about.

I've handled weddings where people take a look at the bottle and say, "Aw, that's so them!" Just make sure you try these "entertainment factor" wines; make sure they taste good and place them throughout the reception venue for all to see.

Wine Even Before the Bride Arrives

There's never a bad time to drink wine on a wedding day, so I suggest you have a big-gun, hyper-expensive bottle of Champagne like *Krug, Dom Pérignon, Cristal* or *Grand Dame* ready in the limo for you, the man of your dreams, your maid of honor and the best man to sip as you travel to the reception. Being your first drink together as a married couple, it should be the absolute best. And as you proceed through life together, that style of Champagne is something you can look forward to year after year on your anniversary. And have Champagne waiting in the cars transporting the rest of the wedding party to the reception. This is a really nice thing to do.

Wines and the Cocktail Reception

If you haven't already noticed, weddings, more than any other group celebration except office Christmas parties, bring out the drinkers. And the heavy-duty imbibing begins during cocktails, no matter whether it's a breakfast, lunch or dinner reception.

Greet the Happy Couple with Champagne

Trust me, wine and spirits trump food for what most people will want when they arrive for your Big Day. If hors d'oeuvres are flying in their faces and there isn't a drink to be had, grumbling will indeed ensue!

Knowing this, it's really nice to have everyone at the reception well prepared with a glass of bubbly before the bride arrives. There is nothing more moving than everyone having a raised glass when the bride and groom arrive at the cocktail reception. I've wondered for years what rule keeps us from informally toasting the bride and groom the moment they arrive at the reception. This lovely, unique touch shouldn't stop anyone from doing another round of formal toasts later on during the wedding meal.

From the Alpana Files:
The Wedding Day Champagne Keepsake

After you have your first Champagne toast with your new husband, ask the maid of honor or best man to autograph and date the bottle with a metallic Sharpie, along with the two of you. You know this is something you will both cherish forever.

Another thing you can do to create a marvelous wedding day keepsake is to take the "first bottle," remove the autographed label (label-removing technology can be found through International Wine Accessories at www.iwawine.com) and have it framed.

Champagne and the vow of love, a truly remarkable pairing!

Light Wines Are Right for Wedding Cocktail Time

For the cocktail reception of your wedding, consider light red and light white wines. In the white category, that means either a Sauvignon Blanc, Pinot Blanc or Pinot Grigio. From the red category, I recommend a Pinot Noir, a Sangiovese or a Barbera. These wines are flexible enough to pair nicely with anything from salty snacks like pigs-in-a-blanket to high-end hors d'oeuvres like *gougeres au truffe noir*, black truffle puff pastries. By the way, alcohol, particularly wine, is a pretty effective appetite enhancer. Keep in mind that if you have a "wine and beer only" cocktail reception, as some do, people will be famished for real food. So keep the wine-and-beer-only reception brief or well-stocked with hors d'oeuvres.

Wines and the Reception Meal

I have managed and attended zillions of different kinds of reception meals from lush breakfasts to monster-sized lunches to grand, multi-course dinners. All in all, no matter what time of day you're going to have a wedding meal, chances are it will be very substantial. For this meal, then, you shouldn't worry about pinpoint accurate food and wine pairing. For the best way to manage this basic wine pairing, refer back to my food and wine pairing guidelines (pp. 95–100).

Wines by the Venue

Party wines, or banquet wines, are usually taken from a different list from what may usually be served at event venues. Party and banquet wine selections are usually less expensive and more mainstream. This doesn't mean they are bad wines. Part of the reason why highly available wines are chosen for large events planned well in advance, is that, as I have said, rarer wines like Silver Oak Cabernet Sauvignon are in limited supply, so banquet venues and restaurants can't keep a large supply of these super wines on hand. Banquet locations try to deal in wines that are reliable and readily available, if not too memorable.

Don't Plan Wine Too Far in Advance

I have already said, but I want to emphasize again, that you should not choose your wines too early. You won't know if the wine will be available, so a less satisfactory substitute may be brought in without your even knowing it, or the flavor of the wine you do want may actually have changed as a result of over aging. And if I've said it once, I've said it a million times: wine is organic and in a state of constant chemical change in smell, texture and taste.

The Reception Calculation—How Much Wine Do You Need?

I repeat, 3/4 of a 750ml bottle per person is the best consumption calculation for wedding receptions. Everybody drinks at weddings, even the aunts who say, "I never drink!"; they ignore their teetotalism once the party gets started. So have plenty of wine on hand for the marriage feast.

A Separate Wine Purchase—a Possible Budget Saver

Find out the venue's policy on laying in wine you independently purchase, because that could save you money on good wines. Let's say you're serving 150 people at roughly 3/4 of a bottle per person (that's 113 total). At most reputable wine retailers, when you buy a significant amount of wine by the case, you can get an additional 10% knocked off each case (there are 12 bottles to a case). Using the 113-bottle total, that adds up to significant savings, since you'll be buying more than 9 cases.

When you visit a wine store to purchase wedding wines, make clear at the outset how much you intend to spend. Next, ask them to outfit you with three good whites and three good reds to take home for a tasting. Take the "test wines" to a BYOB and taste them along with food similar to the wedding meal. Or you could cook what you plan to serve and test the wines at home.

Technically speaking, you are the host of your own wedding, no different from hosting a group of friends who come by for a backyard BBQ. In short, you should be certain you like what you're serving your guests.

One last advantage of buying a large amount of wine from a good wine retailer is that they can deliver the goods efficiently. They have the trucks and know how to get your order to the right place at the right time.

From the Alpana Files:
At Special Events, Bring Wine Down!

Here's a little wine service trick for weddings, or any other social event, for that matter. Whatever wines you plan to serve, bring the temperature down. Chilling certain wines, particularly those with less desirable flavor, can make them easily more drinkable.

Wedding Wine From the Mass Retailer

If you have a tight budget for your wedding, you may want to go to a mass retailer like Sam's Club or Costco for what a friend of mine calls "competent wines that are bound to work." Well, yeah, you can find a good deal at those places because they tend to have pretty capable wine buyers. The problem is transporting the wine. If you need ten or twenty cases, you could lose every dime of savings in the costs of transporting and storing that much wine. Believe me, no venue is going to say, "We'll be glad to store twenty cases of wine two weeks before your event." So please think about this when you consider going to a mass retailer for your wine.

Wine and the Catered Wedding

If you choose to have your affair catered, find out how the caterer will manage your wine and liquor purchases. Once you have their estimates, you may want to compare the caterer's wine numbers with the numbers of a reputable wine retailer. If the caterer is buying from that retailer, chances are the caterer will mark up the wine that you could have gotten at the same price the caterer is paying. There is a slight chance that the caterer's buying power may allow them to get a steeper discount for wine than you could. The question then becomes who gets the savings, capice?

Corkage Fees

If you do choose to bring in your own wine at a restaurant or hotel, find out beforehand if they have a corkage fee, as they do at some BYOB restaurants. The rationale is that the establishment has to supply glasses and chillers, as well as store, refrigerate, open, pour and tend the wine. Corkage fees can start as low as $2.50 a bottle and go as high as $50.00 a bottle at very upscale places. So always inquire in advance about a corkage fee.

No Choice at a Wedding is the Best Choice

Other than being offered "Red or White?" at a reception table, wedding guests should be given little choice of wine. It's highly advisable not to confuse people during this festive time with too many, or complicated, wine choices.

You want the service staff to bring out food, keep wineglasses filled and not have to worry about which wines—of, let's say, four—each guest prefers. There's enough confusion at a wedding reception without adding to it.

If you do choose to have a wine with every course, make certain with the Service Captain that the correct wineglasses will be at the tables and that the servers will pour each wine with the appropriate course.

From the Alpana Files:
Top 10 Signs You've Become a Winezilla!

10. You insist that your bridesmaids refer to the color of their dresses as Merlot, not Maroon.

9. You're mad at your fiancé for having been born in a bad vintage year.

8. During the wedding rehearsal you rate everyone's performance by a point scale. You give the preacher an 85 and the flower girl a measly 60.

7. You let the band have it for not knowing the words to "Red, Red Wine."

6. You have the waiter sent home after he mistakenly referred to the Provençal Rosé as "White Zin."

5. You fire the wedding planner after she says she doesn't drink wine because sulfites give her a headache.

4. You have your mother's bar privileges cut off after seeing her sneak ice cubes into her glass of Chardonnay.

3. Forget Tiffany's, you're registered at a wine shop.

2. You posted your wedding announcement in the classified section of *Wine Spectator*.

1. You sent Robert Parker a wedding invitation and told him it was BYOB.

Christening Party— The Blessed Little Wine Event

The baby has arrived, and it's time for his or her first *public rite of passage* party. Since this party celebrates the beginning of a child's spiritual life, I'd stick to the wine ideas mentioned in the Bridal Shower section, because christening parties are often held early on Sundays. So at this special event everything, including the wine, should be treated in a thoughtful, light and delicate manner.

Confirmations . . . Welcome to Adulthood, but Still No Wine for You!

I'm no theologian, but as I understand it, most of the major religions have a rite of passage ceremony for children when they enter spiritual or chronological adulthood.

A confirmation party should therefore be recognized for what it is: wedding-reception-lite. With guests who are predominantly family and children, you can use the same wine information as in weddings, keeping in mind that people are not likely to drink as much. Use a third-of-a-bottle-per-person consumption figure for confirmations, as opposed to 3/4 of a bottle per person calculation for weddings.

The Anniversary Party— Let the Sentiment Flow, with Great Wines

Anniversary events give us an opportunity to honor a couple who have kept their loving relationship alive. Anniversary parties are also about having a great time with oodles less pressure than a wedding. With these events we focus our budget and our wine selections on having as much sentimental fun as we can.

Here's a wonderful Anniversary Party wine idea that I've used a hundred times. Find a wine that was produced in the year that the couple were married. I've often seen this evoke a tearful or heartfelt reaction from just about everyone present. It may require a little legwork, or time on the Internet, but you can find wines like Madeira, Bordeaux, California Cabernet Sauvignons, Barolos, Barbarescos, Spanish wines, Ports and Sauternes that reflect the mature, fruitful relationship being celebrated. These wines have withstood the test of time, and may have gotten even better over the years. Basically, these wines remain great no matter how old they are.

From the Alpana Files:
About Wines, Age and Relationships

If a wine tastes bad when it's young, then you can be sure it will taste bad when it's aged. That's why you should think about wine aging in terms of relationships. While a wine may be really good now, does it have what it takes for the long haul? As time passes, a good relationship should become easier and more and more comfortable. A long-term relationship with a wine you plan to keep should be no different.

Winery Anniversaries

You can go online and look for wineries celebrating the 10th, 15th, 25th, 50th, even 75th, anniversary of their founding, as many will offer a special wine with a label marking the anniversary year. Then you can make a gift of a wine that matches the couple's anniversary. Or you can decorate the party venue with the anniversary wine bottles. How cool is that?

Fewer, But Better, Bottles

Here's some really good news. Since anniversary parties tend to be smallish affairs, you will have a much better shot at finding a sufficient quantity of rare or older wine. And since you may need only one case instead of the nine cases we calculated for a wedding, you would have the moola to splurge on fewer bottles of something really special.

Cocktails Made with Wine

With all this talk about parties and special events, we certainly should include other wine drinks your guests could enjoy. If you haven't guessed, I'm talking about cocktails made with wine.

When We Drink Cocktails, Just Call Us "Holly"

The "bright young things" of our times must have cocktails. For whatever reason, many people my age think drinking cocktails makes them look sophisticated. This used to be the case with smoking. While I am a committed wine-gal, I admit that the bright young things may be right about cocktails. There really is something about a woman in a black A-line wearing a long strand of pearls and holding a cocktail glass in her manicured hand—it's a major sophisticated "Wow!" Maybe we all want to be like *Breakfast at Tiffany's* Holly Golightly.

Cocktails Change

As times and fashions change, so must cocktails. In some circles, it's important not only to frequent the trendiest restaurant or bar and own the latest "must have" overpriced handbag, but also to know what cocktails, with wine or otherwise, everyone's drinking. While during these early days of the 21st century, no urbane person would be caught dead ordering a Wine Cooler, there are many other wine-based cocktails that are hot commodities with the "cool set."

A Glass of Wine by Any Other Name

Here I am reading the Style Section of *The New York Times* one Sunday morning and I see that at this important fashion event they're serving a new cocktail named the Ecco-tini. I immediately recognize the prefix of the cocktail's name: a Pinot Grigio produced by Gallo Wineries called Ecco Domani. As I read on, my suspicions are confirmed: the Ecco-tini is nothing more than a Martini glass full of Ecco Domani Pinot Grigio with a frozen grape stuck in as the garnish. I ask you, what does this tell us about the need to be ultra-fashionable these days? Anyway, lets move on to some real cocktails that include wine in a loving and satisfying way.

Wine Cocktails That Are Always in Style

Bellinis and Mimosas

The Peach Bellini, like many other classic wine cocktails, has made a significant comeback over the last few years. The Bellini was introduced at Harry's Bar in Venice in 1934. The Bellini, and its better-known fruity cousin (not that there's anything wrong with being "fruity") the Champagne Mimosa have become standard brunch beverages.

Bellini Recipe*

✓ 3 oz Peach Nectar or Peach Puree
✓ 3 oz Champagne or Sparkling Wine
The Bellini is best served in a Champagne Flute glass. First pour in the peach nectar or puree, then add the Champagne. Stir gently, but not too hard, or you will lose the bubbles and crack the delicate flute glass.

Champagne Mimosa Recipe*

✓ 3 oz Orange Juice
✓ 3 oz Champagne or Sparkling Wine
The Mimosa too is best served in a Champagne Flute glass. First pour in the orange juice, then the Champagne. As with the Bellini, stir gently or there goes the fizz.

* Since these two drinks are made with a lot of fruit juice, it's a waste to use good Champagne. Use inexpensive Champagne—moderately priced Italian Prosecco or Spanish Cava—instead.

From the Alpana Files:
Beyond the Bellini & Mimosa

Since the Bellini & Mimosa are basically fruit juice and Champagne, these cocktails can be easily redone with other fruit nectars. Try the following fruit juices mixed with an equal part of Champagne to make some fizzy, fruity fun. Just don't try watermelon. Nothing ever goes well with watermelon except for a bottle of vodka poured into a watermelon at a picnic or backyard BBQ.

For a tasty variation on the Bellini or Mimosa try these juices as an ingredient:

- Apricot
- Pear
- Pineapple
- Mango
- Guava
- Pomegranate

The Champagne Cocktail

Big in the 1930s and '40s, the Champagne Cocktail is all the rage again. At one time it denoted urbanity and sophistication. Times change. Now the Champagne Cocktail has taken on the status of a "lovers' cocktail," frequently requested on Valentine's Day.

Champagne Cocktail Recipe

✓ 1 lump sugar
✓ Bitters (Angostura or Fee Brothers)
✓ Champagne
✓ Lemon twist
✓ Optional: Splash of Cognac
The Champagne Cocktail is best served in a Champagne Flute glass. Start by placing a lump of sugar in the bottom of the glass. Next, add two or three drops of bitters followed by Champagne up to the glass rim. Garnish with a lemon twist.

The Kir & Kir Royale

The Mayor of Dijon, Burgundy, Félix Kir (1876–1968), first popularized this cocktail of Crème de Cassis and Chardonnay at receptions for visiting dignitaries. Although the main ingredient of the Kir, Crème de Cassis (a liqueur made from black currants) had been created in 1841 when it was called the Blanc-Cass, the Kir has become permanently identified with its greatest promoter, Mayor Kir.

Over the years, people began doing makeovers on the Kir. Chardonnay was replaced with Champagne, and the classed-up Kir became known as the Kir Royale.

Kir Recipe/Imperial

✓ 1 tsp. Crème de Cassis or Chambord
✓ 5 oz. chilled dry white wine like Macon Chardonnay
The Kir is best served in a standard 6 oz. wine glass. First pour the Crème de Cassis or Chambord, then add the white wine.

Kir Royale Recipe

✓ 1 tsp. Crème de Cassis or Chambord (with Chambord it is called a Kir Imperial).

✓ 5 oz. sparkling wine or Champagne

The Kir Royale is best served in a tall Flute glass. First pour in the Crème de Cassis, or Chambord, then add the Champagne.

Lillet

Lillet Blanc makes a very refreshing morning, afternoon or evening pre-meal cocktail. Lillet is an orange-flavored French apéritif that has been produced in Bordeaux since 1887. It's made from a base of white wine infused with a secret blend of fruit liqueurs, herbs and spices. Lillet is best served over ice in a Manhattan glass with an orange wheel. The highly flexible Lillet recipe can be adapted to create the more exotic Lillet Mojito.

Lillet Mojito Recipe

✓ 2 oz. Lillet

✓ 6 fresh mint leaves

✓ 1 orange slice (use 2 lime wedges if you want a more traditional Mojito)

✓ 1 tsp. sugar

✓ 2 oz. club soda or lemon-lime soda if you like a sweeter Mojito

✓ Sprig of mint and orange twist

✓ Ice

The Lillet Mojito is best served in a Highball or tall glass. Begin by muddling (crushing) the mint leaves, sugar and orange together until the three ingredients become a slurry. Place the slurry and ice in the glass. Next pour in the Lillet and seltzer or lemon-lime soda. Garnish with a sprig of mint and orange twist.

The Manhattan

Surprise! The venerable Manhattan is another classic cocktail made with wine. For this gem of a drink, the wine needed is Sweet Vermouth, an aromatised wine from Italy.

Manhattan Recipe

✓ 1 3/4 oz. whiskey
✓ 2/3 oz. Sweet Vermouth
✓ 1 dash bitters
✓ maraschino cherry or orange twist
After you shake the ingredients to death in a metal cocktail shaker filled with ice, pour this cocktail on the rocks in a Manhattan Glass (short tumbler) or serve it "up" (no ice) in a Martini Glass. Garnish with an orange twist or maraschino cherry.

The Martini

You do realize, don't you, that a Vodka or Gin Martini is another cocktail made with wine? Supposedly dating back to late 19th century San Francisco, the properly made Martini sparingly uses Dry Vermouth as its second ingredient in addition to either Gin or Vodka.

Martini Recipe

✓ 2 3/4 oz. of Gin or Vodka
✓ 1 to 2 drops Dry Vermouth
✓ Olive(s) or lemon twist
After you shake the heck out of the ingredients in a metal cocktail shaker filled with ice, this cocktail is best served on the rocks in a Manhattan Glass (short tumbler) or "up" (no ice) in a Martini Glass (duh!). Garnish with olives or a twist of lemon.

Note: If you like things "dirty," drop a couple of tea-spoons of olive-jar juice into the shaker when you're making a Martini. The dash of olive juice gives the cock-tail a nice salty finish.

Mulled Wine . . . for the Holidays and Colder Days

Mulled Wine is not so much a mixed cocktail as it is a seasonal spice-enhanced wine. It's kind of a grown-up version of hot apple cider. The Germans call mulled wine *Gluhwein*, while the Swedes call it *Glogg*. A big warm mug of this elixir is especially soothing after braving winter's cold or fighting holiday shop-ping crowds.

Mulled Wine Recipe

✓ 1 bottle of just about any inexpensive red or white wine
✓ 2/3 cups sugar
✓ A cup of Brandy or Cognac
✓ 8 cloves
✓ 1 cinnamon stick
✓ 1 tsp. nutmeg
✓ 1/8 tsp. allspice
✓ 1/8 tsp. dried ginger powder (optional)
✓ zest from one orange

Mulled wine is best served in a nice-looking large ceramic, or thick glass, mug. First, pour an entire bottle of wine into a big non-stick or fire-safe glass pot. Heat the wine over low heat. DO NOT LET THE WINE BOIL! As the wine begins to warm, add the sugar and spices. Stir con-tinually until the sugar is dissolved. Next, add the brandy and orange zest into the mix. Heat the pot's contents thor-oughly for 15 minutes; remember to keep the wine from boiling. Serve warm, and garnish with orange slices or a cinnamon stick.

Raspberry White Wine Spritzer

A classic white wine spritzer is made with club soda and white wine. I like this jazzier version made with fruit and flavored seltzer. It is a perfect summer thirst quencher. You can customize this recipe to fit your own tastes by using any fruit and flavored seltzer water combo you may prefer. I happen to like raspberries.

Raspberry White Wine Spritzer Recipe

✓ 4 oz. light white wine such as Pinot Grigio
✓ 1 oz. raspberry-flavored seltzer water
✓ 2 thin lemon wheels
✓ 4 to 6 fresh or frozen raspberries
✓ Ice cubes

Any spritzer is best served in a large bowled stem glass. Simply pour the white wine and seltzer over the fruit and ice.

Sangria . . . Probably the Coolest "Hot" Wine Cocktail!

Sangria was introduced to Americans by the Spanish government at the 1964 World's Fair. Since then Sangria, at one time a humble farmer's drink, has became a popular party favorite around the world. While Sangria is best known as a red wine-based drink, it can also be made with white wine; it is then called "Sangria Blanco."

Don't just buy a Sangria mix at the store. Have fun and create your own brew. Sangria's appeal is all about taking red or white wine and experimenting with your favorite fruits.

Alpana's Favorite Sangria Recipe

✓ 1 full bottle of red or white wine. For an authentic taste, use a Spanish Red Rioja

✓ 1 each of chopped or sliced orange, lemon, lime, apple and pear

✓ 1 cup of other favorite fruit (sliced strawberries, raspberries, mango, melons, grapes, peaches, etc.)

✓ 1/4 cup white sugar

✓ 1 cup of orange juice (or you can use guava juice, mango juice, tangerine juice, etc.)

✓ 2 cups lemon-lime soda (If you prefer a drier Sangria, use carbonated water instead.)

✓ Ice

Optional

True Sangria has the hard stuff in it. If you want to give the high-octane version a try, add the following to the recipe above:

✓ 1/3 cup of your favorite rum (You can even use different flavored rums, like those with coconut, mango or spices.)

✓ 1/3 cup of Grand Marnier or Cointreau

Sangria is best served in 6 oz. wineglasses. For that fancy Martha Stewart touch, garnish with orange slices on the glass rim. In a large pitcher, combine all the ingredients except the soda. Refrigerate Sangria until well chilled, at least 2 hours or overnight, to allow the flavors to blend. Before serving, pour the Sangria into a pitcher of ice cubes, top with desired amount of soda, garnish with fresh fruit and enjoy. This amount should serve up to six, depending of course on how thirsty everyone is. Have a second pitcher ready, just in case.

The Gift of Wine . . . Don't Sweat It

Over the years, I have received countless inquiries about what wine to bring to someone's house as a gift. It can be stressful enough to attend your boss's dinner party without having to worry about what wine to bring. So let's get rid of some of that stress.

First, follow the position postulated by any good etiquette website, book or maven; the wine you give as a gift is just that, a gift. Put another way, the giver should not expect the recipient to open the bottle right away.

As usual, for every rule there is an exception. If a host puts you in charge of wine for a given event, then you can drink what you bring. If that's the case, you'll need to find out what kind of food the host plans to serve and then, using all the great wine/food pairing tips in this book, you can select an appropriate wine gift.

If you can't decide on a winning wine selection, fear not. I've never met anyone who doesn't like a good dessert wine or Champagne. Both of these make universally acceptable and always appreciated gifts. And you don't have to spend a fortune on the wine gift either, but keep in mind that there is a happy medium between staying within a realistic budget and being a cheapskate. So giving a bottle of something that can be easily recognized and price-checked, can backfire. When I was a sommelier, I remember being asked by a nice couple about a wine gift they had been given. Unfortunately, I was the one who had to break it to them that their friend had probably spent a whopping $4.99 on something that can be found at almost any local supermarket. So be sure and cover your tracks by buying only unique or obscure budget wines that you have tasted or that a retailer recommends.

Champagne . . . the Wine for all Reasons

As I mentioned earlier, some folks are conditioned to think of Champagne as solely a celebratory drink. Nothing could be further from the truth. I have a great friend who dismisses that as outdated thinking and says, "Yes, champagne is a drink for celebration. And lucky for me I celebrate any day that ends in the letter 'y'." She's my kind of woman! You are probably thinking about how Champagne could wreck your budget. Well, there are some good Champagnes and sparkling wines that make great gifts, with prices starting at around $10 to $30 a bottle.

Three budget "sparklers" certain to make a great wine gift include:

- *Spanish Cava*—Segura Viudas Heridad Brut

- *Champagne*—Nicolas Feuillatte Brut

- *American Sparkling Wine*—Argyle Brut Oregon

Dessert Wines Should Be Given with Something Extra

The thought of giving a dessert wine may seem strange, but when given in the right way, the gift will be highly appreciated, and reflect well on you. But I suggest that you also bring a treat for the recipient to enjoy privately. Keep in mind that your host will most likely be exhausted at the end of the evening with nothing to look forward to but post-party cleanup. So what could be a more thoughtful gesture than to give a dessert wine along with a breakfast pastry—brioche or croissant—or chocolates? You could also include a note: "Thanks for throwing a wonderful bash; I hope you enjoy this tomorrow."

Any Old Port Makes Them Warm

There are two kinds of Port Wine that make excellent gifts. The first of these are the deep red *Ruby Ports* with flavors of figs, raisins and blackberries. A box of chocolates and fruit-filled truffles will make an excellent companion to a bottle of *Ruby Port*. The second type of Port Wine is *Tawny Port*, which is aged in barrels for a minimum of seven years. This extended aging process gives the wine its tawny color. The caramel, golden raisin and nutty flavors of this Port go extremely well with almonds, milk chocolate and almost any light-brown or tawny confections and pastries, even oatmeal cookies, pound cake and pecan pie.

Sauternes and Sauternes-like

If you are in the mood to really splurge, buy a bottle of *Sauternes*. Sauternes is a late-harvest dessert wine made from Semillon and Sauvignon Blanc grapes grown in the south of France near Bordeaux. These delectable golden-colored wines are prized for their flavors of honey, apricot and peaches. While the "Chateau" versions of Sauternes can cost as much as a couple of hundred dollars for a half bottle, there are some reasonable alternatives. One of these is Barsac, which comes from a neighboring appellation and is very, very nice. You can also find late-harvest Semillons from other regions, Australia and California among them.

Others Dessert Wine Gifts

From the Tuscany region of Italy, there's a really good dessert wine called *Vin Santo*, or *Saint Wine*, an interesting name derived from a story about a priest having cured sick parishioners with this wine. Tuscans love to have this wine with biscotti. They use the Vin Santo like a sweet dipping sauce, slipping the marvelous Italian cookie in and out of the wine before taking a bite.

Moscato d'Asti is a major crowd pleaser that tastes like apricot and peaches, is low in alcohol and has a little sparkle to it. This wine goes great with peaches and cake desserts.

Color Coordinate Dessert and Wine

I may be a little simplistic here, but I've noticed that the color of a dessert can help you determine the wine with which it should be drunk; a wine corresponding in color. Here is a color code for selecting wines to pair with desserts:

Light-colored, fruit-based desserts—tarts/pies/pastries made with fresh fruit—pair well with golden dessert wines such as late-harvest *Rieslings* and late-harvest *Semillons* like *Sauternes*.

Custard desserts—crème brulée/tapioca/rice pudding and delicate sugary cakes and cookies—pair well with amber and straw-colored dessert wines like *Moscato d'Asti, Muscats, Vin Santo* and *Champagne.*

Dark chocolate desserts—tarts/pies/pastries/cakes/cookies—are easily paired with dark *Ruby Ports.*

Milk chocolate and nut-based desserts—tarts/ pies/pastries/cakes/cookies—pair nicely with light-brown *Tawny Ports.*

Giving a Wine Gift From Afar

If you want to buy someone a nice bottle of wine when he's celebrating a special occasion at a restaurant, here are tips:

Right way

Simply call the restaurant where the wine giftee will be dining and say to the sommelier or the manager, "Buy them whatever they would like. Here's my credit card number." In my years at Everest, no wine gift recipient ever asked me to bring the most expensive thing on the wine menu. They usually asked me to help them choose a wine that would go well with the meal. I always picked something that would be a real fit, but not break the bank. Oh, and remember to ask the restaurant to include an adequate tip in addition to the cost of the wine.

It's Not About You

You probably don't need to be reminded that you should avoid imposing your personal wine tastes on your giftee. If, for instance, she doesn't drink red wine, a gift of red is obviously a potentially expensive bust. My good friend Chris, who is allergic to red wine, was gifted as a surprise with a bottle of *Cakebread Merlot* from afar by a well-wisher. Chris had to say to the server apologetically, "Gee, thanks, but I have to tell you, red wine gives me hives."

Champagne at the Ready

A simple, straightforward way to gift wine from afar is to call the restaurant and ask them to have a bottle of Champagne ready and waiting at your recipient's table.

If you have limited funds, buy a couple of glasses of Champagne to be served as an apéritif. Nothing could be sexier then having two beautiful glasses of Champagne waiting for your giftees when they arrive. Buying them a couple of glasses of dessert wine at meal's end also does the trick nicely. In either case, you make people happy and your thoughtfulness will be appreciated.

From the Alpana Files:
How to Avoid War with France

If you have the good fortune to travel to France and receive an invitation to someone's home for a meal, don't bring wine as a gift. Not surprisingly, all levels of French society consider themselves wine afficionados. By innocently bringing a bottle of wine to a French home, you may be saying to the hosts, "I know more about wine then you do." Bear in mind, by the way, that French people will often give you a drink in their home and then take you to a restaurant for dinner.

All Things Wine

FROM HANDLING TO GLASSES TO GADGETS TO CLEAN-UP

Not quite all things wine are included in this chapter, but there are a lot of great ideas and accoutrements that will enhance your day-to-day wine enjoyment.

Chill to Thrill

I'm on a constant mission to let everyone know that temperature really can either make or break a wine, because we Americans tend to drink our white wines too cold and our red wines far too warm.

Cool Reds

Way back when, before central heating and air conditioning, acceptable room temperature was much lower than it is today. It wasn't between 68° to 73° F., as it is now; it was closer to 55° to 65° F. People obviously wore heavy clothing indoors. Anyway, as it happens, the ideal temperature at which to serve red wine is actually between 55° and 65°. This is the temperature range at which wine producers keep their wine stock, either in naturally cool caves or climate-controlled storage, before shipment. Serving reds closer to the proper cellar temperature heightens the fruit flavor while lessening the alcohol aroma, giving the wine a more vivid structure with focused acidity. If you don't believe me about the alcohol aroma, try this test. Drink warm, rather than chilled, vodka. The warm vodka will smell like rubbing alcohol.

Bring Down Red

You can see what has happened. The conventional wisdom has been that red wine should be served at "room temperature." But red wine served at modern room temperature is way too warm. So what do you do? There are cooling systems that at one time were available only at restaurants and wine bars. If you can afford it, you can now buy one of these systems for your home. At this point, you may well be saying, "I'm not going to pop for a fancy wine cooling system or wine cabinet!" But there is an easy, if not precisely accurate, way to prep your reds to the right temperature.

If you are going to drink red wine, place it in a refrigerator— we'll assume your refrigerator is set at the ideal 37° F—for a solid fifteen minutes before opening it. This will bring the red wine down to where it will really taste great, at about 55° to 65° F.

Warm Whites

When it comes to drinking white wine at the right temperature, there is a helpful rule of thumb. The more expensive or complex a white wine is, the more need there is to drink the wine at a warmer temperature than you would normally do. This will give you the full benefit of a white wine's flavor. White Burgundies and California Chardonnays, for instance, should be served between 50 and 53° F. This allows the delightful creamy texture and complex aromatics of these wines to come through. Chill these wines in your refrigerator, then bring them out about twenty minutes before you serve them, so they will have reached the ideal serving temperature.

From the Alpana Files:
Wine on Display isn't Okay!

In order to get guests to buy wine; many restaurants openly display wine in harshly lit cases. This is not a good practice. Of course racks of wine can be an attractive and enticing part of a restaurant's décor, but letting wine sit under warm lights does nothing for the wine's flavor except to diminish it.

Cooler Whites

You will enjoy a simpler white wine like a Sauvignon Blanc, Pouilly-Fumé, Sancerre or Pinot Grigio, more if they are colder. About one hour in the regular old icebox should put them right where they are most perfect for being served. If you have an emergency and have to chill one of these whites in a real hurry, it's okay, contrary to conventional wisdom, to put it into the freezer for twenty-five minutes or a little longer. While you wouldn't want to *store* wine in the freezer, chilling it in this way is no different from chilling with a wine chiller, a bucket of ice. It's important to set an egg timer or the digital clock on the microwave to remind you that the wine is in the freezer. Otherwise, you may suddenly hear a muffled, deep octave KA-POP! from the wine being at the "Antarctic" freezer setting too long.

Super Cheap Wine, Means Super Chill

If you do end up drinking super cheap white wines, you'll enjoy them much more if you super chill them down.

From the Alpana Files:
Crunchy Wine Tastes Better

To further underscore the reason why simpler white wines should be thoroughly chilled, here's a tasty experiment you can do with grapes. First, put a bunch of grapes into a metal bowl filled with ice water, and place the bowl in the refrigerator. After 15 minutes, take the grapes out and as you bite into the fruit, you will immediately notice that the grape flesh has a pleasant sweetness and is on the crunchy side. What has happened is that the grape acidity, just like the acidity in wine, reacted to the cold in a way that made the grape crisper and more snappy.

For the same reason, you should bring down the lighter or less expensive reds (or almost any red wines that look somewhat translucent) like *Sangiovese, Pinot Noirs,* or *Barberas.* The chilling will brighten the wine's acidity and heighten its fruitiness, giving it a crunchy, rich texture that will make the simpler or less expensive red wine taste richer and fuller. But if you try this with red wines that are heavy in tannins like a *Cabernet Sauvignon, Malbec,* and *Bordeaux,* it will add unwanted richness and makes the wine taste like wine-soaked wool socks.

ALL THINGS WINE   193

Chillin' Out Sparklers

Chilling Champagne is another story altogether. I know I have belabored to death the fact that a bottle of Champagne is under a lot of internal pressure created by the wine's C02 content. Given that, the glass of a Champagne bottle, or any sparkling wine for that matter, needs to be thicker. Since they are in a thicker glass container, it takes longer to bring sparkling wines down to the right temperature. To speed up the Champagne chilling process, get an ice bucket, or a metal bowl that can accommodate water (an essential, because water conducts cold, to get the temperature down faster); place the bottle in the ice water, then either twist the bottle in place or cover the bucket/ bowl with a cloth to concentrate the cold. To really speed the chilling process, place the bottle in the ice water container in the refrigerator. You'll have chilled bubbly in minutes.

Champagne, What's in a Name? A Lot!

You probably know that a sparkling wine can be called Champagne only if it comes from the Champagne region of France. If it comes from anywhere else, it must be called "sparkling wine." Champagne producers, with good reason for all the work they put into this terrific wine product, are intensely protective of this valuable wine's name. Such a good job is done protecting the integrity of Champagne's name that the folks at Prada could learn a lesson or two from Champagne copyright attorneys about how to prevent knock-offs.

Champagne vs. Sparkling Wine. When it comes to Champagne vs. sparkling wine, nothing ever tastes quite like the real stuff. One important reason behind this difference can be found in the ideal soil (or *terroir*) and particular climate where Champagne grapes are grown. The other reason is the process by which Champagne is made.

How Do They Get Those Tiny Bubbles in the Bottles? Where do Champagne bubbles come from? The process to make Champagne is called the *Champagne Methode* or the *Method Champenoise*. Champagne is made using various combinations of Chardonnay and, believe it or not, two red grapes, Pinot Noir and Pinot Meunier. The first step is to make still wine from these grapes. The still wine is then put into a wine bottle with an additional dose of yeast and sugar in order to create the second fermentation. This is what makes this wine-making process unique. Inside the bottle, the yeast will feed on the sugar and give off carbon dioxide, producing bubbles.

Next, with the yeast still in the bottle, the wine must age for a specific length of time. In this part of the process, Champagne develops its distinctive nutty, toasty flavor. After this aging period, the dead yeast is removed from the bottle, and a measured amount of sugar and wine is added to create the Champagne's desired sweetness level. This is called dosage. The bottles are then corked, sealed, boxed and shipped off to ports around the world. As you can see, the Champagne-making process is time-consuming and labor-intensive—hence the high price tag on good French bubbly.

Food and Temperature, from the Obsessive-Compulsive Point of View

Here's another way to look at this wine and temperature thing. A friend of mine always asks servers, when it comes to desserts, "Are your desserts served at room temperature?" While my friend may be a lovable obsessive type, he is right to ask, because desserts that are too cool or warm, except for apple pie and molten chocolate cake, are less flavorful.

Temperature Test

I have heard many people say, "Wine is wine, no matter at what temperature you drink it." If you believe that, open a bottle of wine and drink a small amount at room temperature. Next, if you can stand to wait, put the remaining wine in the refrigerator. After it's been in there for fifteen minutes, take it out and taste it again. If you don't see the difference in taste and texture I want to know—maybe you should consult a specialist to have your taste buds examined.

Wine Must Be Pampered

The next time you go to a wine retailer, notice how the shop stores its wine. If it is done in full exposure to light and at room temperature, you will need to nurse the wine, particularly good wine, back to its organic best health before opening and enjoying it. Quality wines like complex Burgundies or pricier Pinot Noirs just don't like to be yanked in and out of different environments. These wines essentially need to be pampered.

Often, in old movies, a snobbish character will remark that a wine "doesn't travel well." That's what I'm talking about here. Some wines are so sensitive that to get them to settle down, they should be kept for a few days in as controlled and stable an environment as possible. You will be rewarded for this little exercise in patience with good-tasting wine.

Wine Loves a Bad Hair Day

Humidity may be an enemy to your hairdo, but it is a friend to an unopened bottle of wine. A 70% humidity level allows corks to retain moisture and not shrink or crumble.

When Good Wine Goes Bad . . . the Telltales, and What to Do About Them

Oxidation or Madeirized

If a white wine smells like sherry or walnuts and the color is brown rather than a straw yellow, and if a red wine smells like raisins and Madeira and the color is brown instead of red, then they have oxidized or madeirized. Over a period of time, small doses of oxygen are necessary to help a wine mature and age. But too much oxygen can cause the wine to spoil. This is the same chemical reaction you get if you cut open an apple and leave it. After a few minutes, the apple will start to turn brown from oxygen exposure. Faulty corks, exposure to heat and improper storage are the most common causes of oxidation. If this has happened to your wine, you should return it and make another selection.

Sulphur

If the wine in your glass smells like a burnt match or rotten eggs, this means the wine was exposed to a heavy dose of sulphur dioxide. Sulphur is a necessary element to prevent wine from spoiling, but if too much is present in the wine, it can cause these funky smells and can burn the lining of your nostrils. Usually decanting, or swirling, will help blow off this offensive odor.

Sediment

After a length of time in the bottle, red wine will exude sediment that looks like black flakes or specks. This is a natural occurrence and should not be considered a problem: almost all reds eventually throw sediment. Decanting the wine will eliminate the sediment, but if some gets into your glass, in all likelihood it won't affect the wine's flavor. If you do swallow a little sediment, just consider it roughage.

Tartrates or Wine Diamonds

If you happen to notice purple or golden-colored crystals on the bottom of a cork, or in your wineglass, don't be alarmed. It's not glass. These tiny crystals, known as wine diamonds, are a form of *cream of tartar* and are created when wine is exposed to cooler temperatures. For aesthetic reasons, some winemakers cold-stabilize wine to get rid of wine diamonds. Some quality winemakers don't do this, because they believe that cold stabilizing takes away from the wine's flavor. The presence of wine diamonds should be considered a sign of quality.

Brettanomeyces (Brett)

Barnyard or animal aromas in wine can be brought on by a strain of yeast known as Brettanomyces. Wines from Bordeaux and the Southern Rhone are famous for having this characteristic. Some people actually enjoy this aroma; they think it adds character to the wine; others link these smells to dirty winemaking. I guess there are those of us who are into leather and those who are not.

Volatile Acidity

While low levels of volatile acidity (VA) in a wine are okay, excessive amounts of VA can cause wine to smell like vinegar or paint thinner. Decanting wine, or swirling it in the glass, will sometimes eliminate this odor. However, if the smell doesn't go away, by all means make another selection.

If It Fizzes When It Shouldn't . . . It's a Fizzle

If a still wine you are drinking is fizzy or bubbly, and gives off a smell like rotten cabbage, that's more than enough reason to STOP DRINKING IT!

Hanging on . . . to Wine

If you plan to hang on to wine for a while, keep it in a cool, dark place. Leaving wines, other than the simple whites, in a constantly vibrating refrigerator is going, even over a relatively short period of time, to adversely affect them.

People who live in buildings where there may be a below-ground security storage locker or cellar can use these spaces as pretty good wine storage areas.

Wine will do fine stored on a countertop, as long as the heat and glare of sunlight doesn't constantly bombard the bottles.

Wine in Heat

For those who have no cellar access, it's tricky to store wine long term. The choice wine storage for us surface dwellers is usually the back of a closet. This provides a dark place, but clothing insulates against coolness, so closets can become pretty warm. This is not a good thing: long-term exposure to heat accelerates the aging process of wine. In other words, the warmer the area where you store your wine, the faster your wine turns from fun alcoholic grape juice to vinegar.

If you remember your high school physical science classes, you know that all things, animate or inanimate, expand when heated. I have a friend whose wife ordered a bottle of what is one of the best Rosé wines in the world from a very prestigious wine shop in New York City. During shipment, it was inadvertently left too long on a loading dock in 95°F+ temperatures. When the package containing the wine arrived, the inner insulated wrapping was saturated with wine that had leaked through the sides of the cork. This obviously ruined my friend's surprise for her husband.

From the Alpana Files:
Bottle Shock!!!

Bottle shock is what happens to some wines when they are put through the environmental extremes that all living things experience, from traveling by air. Wines put through the torture of air travel will need a few days to settle down after the flight, just as we do when the airlines lose our luggage.

Wine Kept Cool is Wine Forever

Conversely, wine kept at a constant cool temperature retains much of the good that went into making the bottle. There is an interesting story about a Champagne shipment that went down with a ship in the Baltic Sea. Many, many years after the shipwreck the wine was recovered and purchased by chef Charlie Trotter. The opinion of expert tasters was that the wine had held up: its having been in the sea in a cool and constant environment was as if it had been kept in a time capsule. Granted, it had aged, but the effervescence had miraculously remained.

Extreme Environments and Wine

Wine, being a living thing, can be stressed out when exposed to extreme temperatures. This abuse can create spikes in the air pressure within the bottle that literally shocks the wine. This disruption can, and usually does, begin to force the cork outward from the bottle, exposing the cork to the air and ruining the wine.

Say you've laid in a goodly amount of fairly expensive wine. Your investment can be put at risk during hot weather in a home without proper cooling. It's a good idea in that case to move the wine to a consistently cool spot (as close to 55° F as possible) when a heat wave is forecast.

The Constant Wine Storer

While few of us can redesign our homes into the perfect wine preservation environment, there is one thing we can do. If you can take anything away from this section about wine storage, it is key to maintain wine in a constant environment. Even if your wine is at typical room temperature between 68 and 73° F it is better than allowing it to go in and out of extremes.

Sideways

No, I'm not talking about the movie *Sideways* again. I'm talking about the ideal position at which to keep a bottle of wine, and that is *horizontal*. This preventive positioning keeps the cork from drying out. If a cork dries out, it will shrivel and crack, allowing oxygen molecules to get into the bottle and ruin the wine. The really good news is that bottles with the new screw caps can be stored either horizontally or vertically.

Stacked Like Your Shoes

It's easy to store wine horizontally for very brief periods in a refrigerator. But where can you store three to six bottles until the party week after next? Again, as long as it is in a cool dry place, you can stack bottles in one of those wooden or metal wine racks or on a wooden orange or wine crate. Take the crate, knock out the back, put it on its side and stack wine bottles inside it right on top of one another, just as you do with your shoes in your closet.

The Big Wine Storage Question

When you're thinking about keeping wine at home, you need to ask yourself a question: how does my lifestyle relate to wine? I usually buy bottles costing around $10 to $15 and drink them almost immediately. If I want a really expensive bottle of wine, I'll try a glass of it at a wine bar or give it a whirl at a good restaurant. I'm not a wine collector, I have no plans to lay away wine for years to come.

But if you are serious about collecting wine, you should consider some of the home cooling and storage systems currently available at many retail outlets like Sam's Club, Home Depot, Lowe's, Costco, Linens 'n' Things and Bed, Bath and Beyond. These cellar-temperature systems come in sizes from a dorm refrigerator holding only 25 bottles, to custom-built, room-sized floor-to-ceiling mahogany cabinets that can hold hundreds of bottles. You might also want to Google "wine storage" and you will have more choices than you could ever imagine.

While not Optimal, Any Old Glass Will Do For Wine

Okay, here it is. While it matters greatly to millions of wine lovers and others, technically speaking, you can drink wine from any kind of glass, whether it's a Margarita goblet, a Martini glass, a thick plastic baby tumbler or a Dixie cup. Virtually any drinking receptacle, except those made of metal, will not injure a wine's flavor. You know about not drinking from metal because almost any beverage, even Diet Coke, tastes a whole lot better coming from anything other than aluminum. But I have to say that glasses specifically designed for drinking wine, will enhance wine's taste.

Wineglasses Reflect Your Lifestyle

What you basically want in wine glassware is a design and practicality that reflects your lifestyle. Before you select any design, think through how you will treat your glassware. If you're a little clumsy or like to toss things into the dishwasher, you will want glassware that is heavier, thicker, with shorter stems or the tumbler style that is growing in popularity. It's interesting that, a while back, the venerable glassware maker Riedel caused an uproar when they introduced the stemless glass, a design originally intended for urbanites who lack the ample storage area required by space-eating stemmed glassware.

If you want the glass you pour wine into to express your good taste and high quality of life, you can allow yourself the lower weight, longer stemmed glassware that whispers "elegant simplicity." Just keep in mind that the more delicate and taller models must be washed and dried by hand.

A Rose by Any Other Name is a Wineglass?

Roses and wineglasses have something in common. Both have stems for roughly the same reason. Forgetting photosynthesis and all that for a moment, the stems of roses and wineglasses allow the most important feature of the object, the flower or the bowl of the glass, to remain untouched. In the case of the rose, touching the petals may damage the blossom. Similarly, cupping the bowl of a glass of wine in your hands will heat and in all likelihood have a negative impact on the wine's flavor.

Hot Little Hands Off the Bowl!

We all like to think of ourselves as hot stuff. Every inch of our skin radiates a very toasty 98.6° F body temperature. This natural body heat can warm up the bowl of a stemmed glass almost as fast as the time it takes a microwave oven to make popcorn. With that, my hot little friend, I highly advise holding a wineglass by the stem.

Thickness Matters

The real difference in the quality of wine glassware is determined by the thickness of the glass. In most cases, the thinner glass is the better quality, and, unfortunately, the more expensive.

"Come Drink Me" Wineglasses

Your choice of the stem length of wine glassware could be compared to your choice of shoes! (I knew I could work in another mention of shoes if I tried.) Some people prefer jazzy high heels made of super-thin expensive leather—(I call them *taxi shoes*, that hot pair of dress shoes that kill your feet if you wear them longer than two hours, but that look great stepping out of a taxi.)—while others prefer low heels and flats or, as Grandma would call them, "sensible shoes." Then again, some of us wear both. If you buy the full range, as I do with both shoes and wine glassware, depending on the day, mood and occasion, you should bring out the appropriate style.

The Fab Four . . . in Glasses

If you are beginning to take wine very seriously, want to show that you know the correct glasses to serve wine in, or just want to enhance your everyday wine-drinking experiences, I strongly suggest that you have at least six each of what I call *The Fab Four*: the 6-Ounce, the Bowl, the Flute and the Bordeaux. They will accommodate just about all the wines you're likely to drink in a lifetime. If you happen, like me, to be a klutz, you buy six so that in case of breakage you have spares.

The 6-Ounce Wonder

You'll probably put the most drinking mileage on the 6-ounce wineglass. This trusty workhorse will rise to the occasion when you're enjoying the everyday whites like Sauvignon Blanc, Chardonnay, Pinot Blanc and Pinot Grigio, and the light reds like Beaujolais and Rosé.

Bordeaux is Not Just a Place Where They Make a Lot of Wine

The heavy tannic reds such as Merlot, Shiraz, Syrah, Bordeaux, Cabernet Sauvignon, Malbec, Brunello di Montalcino, Cote du Rhone, Pinotage and the Argentinians are best enjoyed in a Bordeaux glass. These wines need a straight-sided glass so that when the wine is swirled to bring out its nose, there's plenty of side-surface area for the wine to climb in order to catch O2. The swirling of a wine in a Bordeaux glass does the same thing that a fabric softener does to rougher cloth

(I know. While accurate, not the sexiest metaphor in the world). Wine swirled in a Bordeaux glass will soften the rich texture that tannins create. When properly swirled in a Bordeaux glass, wines become smoother, so that they go down ever so nice and easy.

From the Alpana Files: Swirl Girls Take Manhattan

Once I was on business in New York City with my best friend Belinda, also a sommelier.

During some free time, we didn't sightsee: we went shopping for wine at what is arguably one of the world's finest wine shops. While we walked up and down the aisles looking at wines that made us tear up with excitement, a floor attendant offered us both a glass of a red that, while truly marvelous, definitely needed swirling. As we did the swirl thing, the retailer said condescendingly, "Oh, I see somebody must have taken a wine tasting class." After we reached into our bags and handed him our business cards, there was an air-sucking hush, and he turned a satisfying deep red.

Sniffing the Bowl

The Bowl wineglass (roughly 12 ounces) is the best choice when you really want to bring out, and enjoy, wine's aroma. Get yourself a Zinfandel, Grenache, Pinot Noir, Rioja or Barbera and fill a Bowl glass about a third of the way full and inhale deeply through your nostrils. You'll have an immediate glorious experience.

Overfilling one of these bathtubs lessens the wonderful smell of the wine. Also, with all the weight created by too much liquid, the glass becomes risky to handle. If you fill the Bowl glass up to the rim, you become a major wine stain just dying to happen.

Flutes and Bubbles

It's appropriate that my favorite of the *Fab Four* wine-glasses is called a Flute, as the name connotes the simple elegance of both the lovely musical instrument and the glass, which is not only beautiful, but also a highly practical design for a glass that holds Champagne.

When drinking Champagne, you don't want too many bubbles, or too few. If you use a glass other than a Flute for Champagne, chances are it has a great deal of bottom surface. Too much bottom surface kicks up the bubble-producing velocity of Champagne, allowing the wine's "fizz" to escape in no time. Low fizz in Champagne means low feel. When the feel from Champagne is gone, it is indeed flat and should be poured only down the drain. The Flute has little bottom surface area, so the bubbles come up at a steady rate. The Flute glass gives you a chance to properly focus on Champagne, the most attractive and active of all wines.

I'll Have a Breast of Champagne, Please

The story is that a woman's breast was used as a model for the now re-emerging Saucer Champagne glass. You've seen this type of glass many times in old movies: scenes where bluebloods in full New Year's Eve regalia toast each other in Champagne.

The Saucer is sometimes referred to as the *Marie Antoinette*, a reference to the story that this unfortunate Queen of France demanded that her Champagne glass be fashioned to fit her breast. This is probably just a legend, like her having said, "Let them eat cake," when she was told that the people had no bread. In any case, over the last few years this wineglass has been making a comeback. It's being used at more and more bars for fussy drinks and Champagne Cocktails. The Saucer glass, while dramatic and quite lovely, with its vast bottom area, will cause massive effervescence. This will accelerate the wine's becoming flat much faster than Champagne in a Flute glass. So, if you're going to drink bubbly from "Marie A.'s breast," knock it back fast before it loses its fizz.

Wineglasses . . . Buying Cheapos, Care and Cleaning

For friends who insist on having real wineglasses at large grazing-style parties, I suggest they put the good glassware away and go to Target, Costco, or any mass retailer and buy six-ounce glasses (a dozen to a box) that can cost as little as $1.25 a piece, or even less. There are two reasons for this. First, who cares if a cheap glass gets broken? Second, the cheaper glassware can handle the force and abrasive power of an automatic dishwasher a lot better than fine glassware. *FYI—leaded crystal can be scratched by dishwasher detergent smashing into it at high speeds.* Unless you're having a really nice sit-down dinner party, or a group of your closest friends, don't put out good wine glassware. People, particularly in large groups, often treat wine glasses with little respect.

Clean Glassware for the Queen

If you're putting out good wineglasses in anticipation of the arrival of your soon-to-be mother-in-law, you'll want to make sure the glassware looks perfect. The best way to wash it is by hand, using a mild detergent or one of those self-contained baby-bottle-washing brushes,that have a small sponge at one end of a handle that can be filled with dish detergent. Use the hottest water possible, because the hotter the water, the quicker the glasses will dry. If you must dry fine glassware immediately, use lint-free cloths, never, of course, paper towels.

A Tool That Helps File Glassware for Another Day

So you end up buying some nice wine crystal glassware like Riedel, Waterford, Webb, Baccarat, Lenox, Depression or Carnival, and what happens? It gets chipped! Before you go into meltdown about having to buy expensive replacements, get your hands on a Glass & Crystal Saver Tool. This clever glassware chip remover is a multi-tasker, as it also works on many glass and crystal items like bowls, vases, dinnerware and decorative pieces.

In a world where guests will treat your "fine ware" like Dixie-ware, this gadget allows you to bring out the good stuff without a second thought.

Check out www.wineenthusiast.com for glass & crystal-saver tool details.

Where the Heck is My Corkscrew?

It amazes me that with so many corkscrews in my world, when I really need one, I can never find any. If you live in a world like mine, you want to just get the bottle open as soon, and with as little fuss, as possible. If that's the case, I'd say the corkscrew for you is the Rabbit. It's called the *Rabbit* because when extended for de-corking action, it looks sort of like a long-eared bunny.

An authentic *Rabbit* corkscrew is not cheap. However, the price of a real *Rabbit*, as opposed to one of the many look-alike knockoffs, is worth the price because they're so easy to operate. Unfortunately, the *Rabbit* is somewhat awkward to pack in a picnic basket.

There are also very cool-looking decorative corkscrews by *Rogar*. Corkscrews from the *Rogar* line, which can be much more expensive than a *Rabbit*, come with their own stand or can be fastened to a butcher-block kitchen island. *Rogars* tend to be pretty large, too. Having a *Rogar* will clearly indicate to visitors that you are a "wine person."

There are other corkscrews available under the popular brand names of *Metrokane* and *Screwpull* (not touching that!). I personally like the smaller *Screwpull* since it fits nicely in a pocket or handbag.

When you are ready to select your corkscrew, make sure it's made of metal and not plastic. You need physics on your side when you remove a cork and metal will give you the leverage and strength that potentially breakable plastic does not.

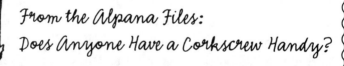

From the Alpana Files:
Does Anyone Have a Corkscrew Handy?

Sixty-eight percent of American households *do not* have a corkscrew. A corkscrew, therefore, could be the one wedding gift they won't return. And until wine bottles go totally screw cap, or you give up wine entirely (not a good idea), you're really, really gonna need one!

Foilcutters

Did you ever wonder what the foil strip covering the neck and cork of a bottle is for? A long time ago these protective strips (they were made then of lead) were intended to prevent mice from eating through the cork and spoiling the wine.

See wineracksplansandmore.com for corkscrew and foil cutter details.

Bottle Coolers . . . Keeping the Chill

Getting wine cooled down quickly, or keeping it cool, has become a lot easier with the help of state-of-the-art cold-pack technology.

Bringing Wine Down Fast the Newfangled Way

The people at *VacuVin* make a wide variety of clever wine gadgets that you should probably look into. One of the best is called the *Rapid Ice Cooler*. This is basically a short plastic sleeve filled with quick freeze chemicals. The RIC easily fits over virtually any standard 750ml wine bottle. After the RIC has had a chance to freeze up, all you do is slip it over a bottle, and the wine is chilled within five minutes. The RIC will also keep an already chilled bottle cool for hours. RICs come in several decorative bottle-coverings.

Marble Cool

In its natural state, marble is cool to the touch, making it good material for controlling a wine bottle's temperature. While a pure marble bottle cooler cannot cool down a bottle of wine, it will help maintain the temperature of a pre-chilled bottle. Marble bottle coolers can be on the heavy side, but they are awfully handsome, so you might want to keep one on hand for special-occasion wine drinking.

Cold Metal

The days of metal wine chillers requiring ice have, for the most part, come to a merciful end. With sophisticated cooling technology like that used to create the VacuVin Rapid Ice Cooler, you can now find a plethora of attractive metal wine bottle coolers. Most of the models simply need to be brought down in a freezer before use.

No Clay Feet With Terra Cotta

With their attractive clay color and quaint appearance, terra-cotta bottle coolers can enhance an appetite for wine. While using old-fashioned technology, terra cottas are very efficient at keeping wine chilled. All you do is fill the terra-cotta bottle chiller with cold water, let the water remain for a minute or so, then pour it out. The porous nature of the clay will hold enough water to maintain a moist, cool environment inside the cooler. This damp, cool place will then keep a bottle of wine chilled at the exact temperature at which it was placed for an hour or so. Of course, you will have to pre-chill the bottle before placing it in the terra-cotta cooler.

Acrylic is So Plastic

Unless you're super-careful, acrylic bottle coolers tend to get scratched up pretty easily. In order to function, most acrylic models also require ice; they have little insulation to keep heat out and coolness in, so if you use the acrylic cooler, you may find yourself going often to the automatic icemaker for a refill.

See wineracksplansandmore.com for bottle cooler details.

Put a Cork, or Better Yet a Screw Cap in It!

I love wine bottles with screw caps instead of natural corks, for many reasons. For one thing, a bottle of wine with a screw cap is much easier to open than one with a natural cork, particularly after you have had your nails done.

Anyway, as I said, with forty corkscrews at home, I can never seem to find a corkscrew when I need one. I can get to the wine faster with screw caps and not kill a valuable half-hour of drinking, looking for a corkscrew.

The most important reason why I love screw caps is because they eliminate the risk of the wine being "corked." I'm not talking about the tiny bits of cork that you may sometimes see floating in your wine, but rather the mold and wet cardboard smell of a bad bottle of wine. This happens when natural cork becomes infected with *cork taint*, a serious problem for the wine industry. And now, with modern screw-cap technology, you won't have to keep your fingers crossed every time you open a bottle of wine.

Wine industry experts believe that anywhere from 5%-10% of all wine sealed with natural cork is infected. Everyone from producers to distributors to retailers to restaurateurs to consumers can be victims of corked wine. Screw caps eliminate the "corked" problem entirely, so you can understand why more and more wineries have chosen to use screw caps and more and more wine-loving consumers are embracing them.

The World Wildlife Fund has recently predicted that in ten years cork could account for as little as 5% of the wine market.

Wine Returned Due to Product Failure

If your wine is corked, go ahead and return it; the retailer should find the wine's being corked to be a completely legitimate reason for the return because the product has indeed failed. Most shops will give you a refund or a new bottle.

Decent Wine Leftovers

If you have a little wine left in a bottle with a screw cap, tighten the cap and pop it in the fridge. This is not perfect, but it's better than shoving a cork back in, because it will limit the amount of air getting at the leftover wine. If screw caps become universally accepted among wine producers, it could save you the expense of buying the wine preservation devices that I mention here.

The De Canter Codes

According to *Merriam Webster*, *decanter* is a noun and refers to "a glass vessel used to hold wine." The *Larousse* French Dictionary calls *décanter* a verb meaning "to allow to settle down, to become clear." Well, both definitions are correct. A decanter is a glass vessel used to hold wine so the wine has time, in one manner or another, to settle down.

Old Wine is New Again

The first of the two kinds of wine that are better when decanted are old wines. Old wines, after being in the bottle for a long time, can develop sludge and sediment that needs to be separated out before the wine can be drunk. If you've ever had Turkish coffee, you know the need to separate the liquid from the fine coffee grounds at the bottom of the Turkish coffeemaker. You do this by carefully pouring the clear coffee from the coffee carafe into a cup. The decanting of older wines works the same way. You slowly pour the wine from the bottle into the clear vessel, managing all the time to keep the dark sediment out of the decanter. Once this is done, the wine is ready to be poured from the decanter into glasses.

At upscale restaurants, you will often see sommeliers decanting wine. The sommelier will usually hold the bottle above a candle, managing not to warm the wine, as he or she pours it into a glass carafe or decanter. The candle has a practical, not romantic, purpose. It is used to illuminate the wine's flow, allowing the sommelier to detect any sediment entering the bottle's neck. When sediment is spotted, the sommelier will gently pause the pour until the bottle sediment settles to where it can be kept from entering the decanter.

If you are decanting an older wine, handle it carefully, otherwise you risk disturbing the sediment and making the process more difficult. Have you ever wondered why you occasionally see some wines carried in a basket? A wine basket keeps the bottle still so the sediment is less likely to be disturbed.

Remember, in decanting older wines, that the aroma of older wines is generally more fragile than that of younger wines. Overexposing older wines to oxygen can therefore quickly diminish one of the things we most enjoy about wine: its aroma. Knowing this, decant older wines close to a time you plan to drink them. Then you can enjoy the wine aromatics longer.

Young Reds . . . Give 'em Plenty of Air

Decanting is also a good way to enhance young red wines. While too much exposure to air spoils the aroma of decanted older red wine, the young reds get better when exposed to air. Next time you open a young red wine, taste it before you take a full pour. If the wine is real "grippy" with intense tannins and is tight in the mouth, that's the sign that the wine needs air through decanting, to become softer in feel and stronger and more pronounced in aroma.

Essentially, decanting a young red allows air to pass through the wine, greatly improving it. The effect of getting air into a young red is very similar to the effect of yoga breathing exercises on the muscles of a human body. Yoga breathing exercises help to get muscles more O2, allowing us to go from tightness to relaxation. It's the same thing with decanted young red wine.

As we've said, older wines need to be decanted in order to separate the wine from the sediment, while younger reds need to be decanted to soften the tannins and release the aromatics. But a decanter should never be used to store wine. Spirits like scotch whiskey will keep in a stoppered decanter, but *wine will not*.

The more delicate older wines (10+ years) shouldn't get too much air. Long-term exposure to air actually flattens these wines out to the point where they lose flavor. I just gave you a good reason to gulp down older reds faster, didn't I?

A Small Price is All You Need to Pay

You don't need to make yourself crazy over purchasing a de-canter. There are models that cost as little as $30 up to $300 and more. No matter what a decanter's cost, they all pretty much do the job equally well. Decanters come in all shapes, styles and designs: for some reason, those shaped like ducks are very popular.

Use a Big "D"

Decanters should be able to hold at least two bottles, or 1500 ml, of wine. This ample size allows for greater air exposure than a 750ml wine bottle could ever provide. Also, the decanter's mouth should be wide enough for you to comfortably pour the wine in without its dribbling. The large decanter will also be wide enough to permit wine being poured into it to "sheet down" the sides. As wine sheets down the decanter's sides, it gets a good healthy dose of oxygen.

From the Alpana Files:
The Heavy Breather

A little air does do wine some good. But I don't agree with what I call the Heavy Breather wine snob who insists that you must wait precisely 22.5 minutes before drinking a decanted wine.

I've even known some Heavy Breathers to stubbornly insist that removing the cork from a bottle and letting it breathe will properly oxygenate the bottle. What these wine zealots don't know is that simply removing the cork does not allow enough oxygen to get to the wine. Wine is better if simply poured right into the glass

Outfitting Wine for the Great Outdoors . . . Wine Carriers & Totes

Whether you plan to dine on the patio, have a picnic at the park or eat hanging from the side of a mountain, you can easily keep wine chilled outdoors with fun modern technology.

Packing Ice Keeps Wine Nice

Many wine carriers, like those made by Louis Vuitton and Gucci, or the Connoisseur Wine Bag from International Wine Accessories, come with detachable ice packs. You simply toss the ice packs in the freezer before use and in no time they freeze up. Once the ice packs are ready for use, place them inside the carrier's ice pack compartments and off you go to the great outdoors. These carriers do okay for a while, but don't delay drinking the wine because after a few hours they will start to lose their chill.

Wine Carriers Built for Fun and Fashion

Built NYC make wine carriers and a whole line of other non-wine carrier goods, that are made from the material SCUBA divers and surfers wear to protect themselves from water's chill. These carriers offer some insulation for wine that has already been chilled, but they can't give you the long-term chill advantages of carriers with detachable ice packs. While functionally not as good as carriers with ice packs, *Built NYC's* wine carriers double as decent fashion accessories, because they come in a variety of trendy colors. I guess to some degree they offer fashion over function. For more information visit http://www.builtny.com/.

For the Wine Bag With No Ice Packs

If you have no ice packs, you can use frozen plastic water bottles to line whatever bag you may use to carry wine. And as the bottles thaw, you will have water to drink as well. Please learn from my mistake and avoid freezing bottles containing carbonated water. Once I accidentally froze bottles of sparkling water and they exploded in my freezer. So freeze only bottles of still water.

It's in the Wine Bag

You can go to almost any wine retailer or department store and find plenty of great wine carriers and totes. If you want to look online, you can visit http://store.thewinebag.com

No Wine Stain Left Behind

If you're as clumsy as I am, you will inevitably spill red wine on a light fabric or on your "good" clothes. Here are a few ways to get the red out!

Wine Away—A very reliable wine-stain-removal product. You can use it directly on the wine mess you've made, whether it's on clothing, carpeting or upholstery. Simply spray Wine Away over the area to be cleaned, wait 30 seconds and rub the stain out. It's that easy! This bleach-free formula is made from fruit and vegetable extracts, so as well as being environmentally friendly, it's safe for use around children and pets. In addition to online access to this great stuff, Wine Away can be found at most wineries, wine shops or quality grocery stores like Whole Foods.

OxiClean—This is pretty good; its only drawback is that it does not work immediately. You need to rinse the stained garment in cold water, pour some OxiClean on the stain and then launder the garment with a capful of OxiClean along with your regular detergent. Find Oxi-Clean at any grocery or home store in America.

Patty's Homemade Formula—This is just that—you make it at home yourself. Patty's Formula is a fairly foolproof way to remove wine stains from laundered fabrics. You mix dishwashing liquid soap with hydrogen peroxide, pour the mixture on the stain and let it sit as a pre-soak. Regardless of the stained item's color, you'll actually see the red wine disappear as you drizzle the mixture on the stain. Works on older stains too. Make sure, however, that the soap/peroxide mixture is relatively fresh. I used some recently that was a few months old (wine being a constant stain hazard in the Singh household, I keep a bottle handy on my washing machine) and it did not completely remove a particularly large stain as it usually does. After I mixed and applied a fresh batch, presto! it worked like a charm.

By the way, for Patty's Homemade Formula to work, it doesn't need much soap. Peroxide should be the dominant ingredient.

White Wine vs. Red Wine . . . White Wine Wins

Here's one that for some reason freaks people out. Dabbing white wine on a red wine stain will remove a lot of the stain. Don't ask me the chemical reason why this happens, it just does.

WINE STAIN REMOVAL WARNING

Soda water, salt and hairspray do *not*, repeat, *do not* work on wine stains. All these substances do is spread the stain to a larger area, if that.

One Last Pour

HAD ENOUGH WINE YET?

No? Good, because there are still plenty of wines coming out every day to buy and try. Because of the exponential growth and popularity of wine, there are a lot of books with comprehensive lists of wines to study and consider. This book, as you now know, is not one of those. I just wanted you to have some fun learning about wine, and to protect you from selection shock. So I have deliberately kept my suggestions toward generic type and variety rather than toward specific wines. I hope this will help you to select the wines that best fit you and your lifestyle.

It's not You—It's the Wine

Once during my "floor years," I served a charming couple who were celebrating their anniversary. After chatting about wine for few moments, they decided to take me up on my recommendation of Zinfandel. I presented the bottle, they tasted it, looked at each other for approval and in unison said, "It's fine." I walked away from the table thinking to myself, Good job, Alpana, another satisfied customer. Well, a half-hour later the couple's server came over to me and said, "The Zinfandel couple would like to see you."

Back at their table, I could see that they had already drunk half the bottle, and I anticipated a compliment on my skilled wine suggestiion. Instead, they said the wine tasted funny and asked me to taste it. I thought, Gee how bad could it be? I took a sip and almost gagged. The red Zin that I had talked up so enthusiastically was not only acrid—it was also sparkling! Gross! I asked why they hadn't said something sooner? They said, "You're the expert, we figured it was us and that's how the wine was supposed to taste."

I felt terrible about it. I assured them, and I assure you, that if you ever think there is something wrong with a wine, chances are pretty good that there is. Unlike the couple in my story, don't be intimidated about speaking up and having the wine replaced; after all, you're the one paying for it. So remember, it's not you, it's the wine.

Alpana's "No Rules" Approach

After years of suggesting wine/food pairings that follow all the rules and regulations, guidelines and mantras that are pretty certain to work, I find it can still boil down to the fact that some people simply don't like red wine or don't like white wine. Ultimately, you must like the wine that you drink and drink the wine that you like. This is the essence of *Alpana's No Rules Approach*.

You've been reading a lot about safe bets throughout this book. However, don't let me or any other wine professional stop you from making your own choices. The most important consideration is that you like and enjoy the taste of a particular wine. But before you reject something on the first try, you need a second taste to be certain whether or not you will enjoy it.

The last thing I want to do is tell you what you must drink. Rely on your own taste. Just please remember to remain flexible: if you do, a whole world of new flavors, interests and interesting people may open up to you.

From the Alpana Files:
Having a Long-Term
Relationship with Wine

Here's a way to have a little fun with a wine while learning what positive effects aging can have.

As a long-term gift to yourself, buy a case (12 bottles) of wine you know and enjoy. Then, on the same day every year until the wine is gone, take one bottle out to enjoy alone or with company. Keep a notebook handy and record how the wine tastes each year, as well as what was going on in your life when you drank the wine. Thus you will create a wine diary that will amuse and teach you a little about yourself, your friends (track how many engagements, marriages and divorces happen in the span of just four bottles. It will freak you out!) and wine in its ever-changing states.

Me Talk Wine pretty One Day

Throughout this book I've encouraged you to go to wine tastings and chat it up with wine professionals at restaurants, event venues and retail stores.

While I've been yammering on about a lot of wines, I haven't told you how to pronounce their names, in case you don't already know. Having this basic skill will make you feel more confident; the newly minted wine impresario.

For your wine edification, here then are phonetic wine pronunciations by category . . .

Sparkling Wines
- Champagne (sham-PAIN)
- Prosecco (Pro-sec-oh)
- Cava (CAH-vuh)

Light White Wines
- Sauvignon Blanc (So-veen-yawn Blonk)
- Pinot Grigio (PEE-noe GREE-joe)
- Gruener Veltliner (Grew-ner Felt-lee-ner)
- Pinot Blanc (PEE-noe Blonk)
- Pinot Gris (PEE-noe Gree)
- Chenin Blanc (Shay-nun Blonk)
- Graves: a.k.a. White Bordeaux (Grahv)
- Sancerre (Sahn-sehr)
- Pouilly-Fumé (Poo-yee Foo-MAY)

Sweet White Wines
- Riesling (REESE-ling)
- Gewürztraminer (Geh-VERTZ-trah-mee-nur)
- White Zinfandel (Zin-fan-dell)
- Vouvray (Voov-ray)
- Sauternes (So-tairn)

Heavy White Wines
- Chardonnay (Shar-doe-nay)
- Viognier (Vee-ohn-yay)
- White Rhones (Rone)
- Marsanne (Mahr-sahn)
- Roussanne (Roo-sahn)
- Pouilly-Fuisse (Poo-yee Fwee-SAY)
- Semillon (Say-mee-yon)

Rosé
- Rosé (Roe-ZAY)

Light Red Wines
- Pinot Noir (PEE-no-Nwahr)
- Gamay (Geh-MAY)
- Barbera (Bar-bear-ah) d'Alba (dahl-bah)
- Sangiovese (San-jo-vay-zay)
- Beaujolais (Bo-zho -LAY)

Spicy Red Wines
- Zinfandel (Zin-fan-dell)
- Shiraz (Shee-rahz)
- Syrah (See-rah)
- Cotes du Rhone (Kote-do-Rohn)
- Rioja (Ree-OH-ha)

Heavy Red Wines
- Cabernet Sauvignon (Kab-ur-NAY So-veen -YAWN)
- Merlot (Mare-LOW)
- Malbec (Mal-bek)
- Bordeaux (Bore-DOH)
- Cabernet Franc (Kab-ur-Nay Fronk)

Alpana's Oenoscope

WHAT'S YOUR WINE SIGN?

Capricorn — Malbec

The sign of Capricorn is a lone goat astride a mountain summit. The ambition and perseverance it took to make this hazardous climb is synonymous with the "die trying" nature of those born under this dynamic sign. The solo climb to the top is reminiscent of Malbec which, after decades in the shadows of other wines, is finally breaking out and gaining serous attention for its deep fruit and full-bodied structure. Come hell or high water, Malbec has, like those born under Capricorn, managed to make it to the top.

Aquarius—Wines with the grenache grape

Aquarians are broad-minded individuals who enjoy the camaraderie of others. Their wide circle of friends come from diverse backgrounds, but to be an Aquarian's friend you must contribute to the betterment of the group. Grenache represents this ideal and is often blended with other grape varieties for balance, finesse and flavor. In the Rhone, Grenache will be blended with Syrah or Mourvedre, and in Spain, Grenache intermingles well with Tempranillo to produce Rioja. Grenache's versatility, like the Aquarians' energy, makes the world of wine a better place to be. So you Aquarians out there should look for blended wines with the grape variety Grenache.

Pisces—Chardonnay

The symbol for Pisces is two fishes swimming in opposite directions; it represents duality. Pisceans are compassionate, sympathetic and sensitive to the moods of people around them. They are emotionally connected to their surroundings and will adapt their nature to accommodate the feelings of others. This is very much like Chardonnay, which will change according to where the source grapes are planted and how the final product is made. So Chardonnays can sometimes be light and crisp, at other times full-bodied and buttery or even fizzy and toasty. Perfect for the sign of the fish.

Aries—Shiraz

Aries, or "the Ram," are anything but sheep-like. They are ambitious, aggressive and full of enthusiastic energy. Aries are also very impatient and impulsive. They aren't likely to hang around waiting for a wine to age until it reaches its optimum maturity. And who can blame them? They want their wine and they want it now! Therefore, ready-to-drink Shiraz, with its expressive fruitiness, is the perfect wine for those born under this sign. With few exceptions, Shiraz is drinkable right after purchase and requires no aging to soften tannins. Aries, being natural-born leaders, will proudly show novice wine lovers that Shiraz has revolutionized the wine world, that you don't have to pay very much for it, or wait too long to drink it.

Gemini—Pinot Grigio/Pinot Gris

Hello Gemini . . . are you both listening to me? I say that because those born under the sign of the twins often have dual personalities. Gemini can be one personality one moment and an entirely different one the next. This quality makes them very interesting, adaptable and versatile. Variety is the spice of life for Geminis and if they could, they would love to be in two places at once. This duality brings to mind Pinot Grigio and Pinot Gris. Although these wines are from the same grape, each represents a different flavor profile depending on where it is grown. Italian style Pinot Grigio is light and crisp while French style Pinot Gris is full-bodied and sometimes sweet. Geminis can also be a little gossipy. If you have friends who like gossip—and who doesn't?—ask them what their signs are and what wine they enjoy, I'll bet they're a Pinot Grigio- or Pinot Gris-lovin' Gemini.

Taurus—Bordeaux

Taurus "the bull" represents stubbornness and an unwillingness to change. Security is extremely important to Taurans, who are not very likely to move once they've established roots. Taurans also have an extravagant side, and are fond of the finer things, particularly good food and wine. With its centuries-long legacy and greatly heralded reputation, Bordeaux is the ideal wine for those born under this sign. Bordeaux represents the best of the Old Guard: Bordelaise winemakers are notoriously stubborn about changing methods or techniques. Even after decades of aging, the wine is reluctant to change. Taurans will appreciate the constancy, stability and reliability of wines from Bordeaux. With Bordeaux wine, Taurans will be overjoyed that they'll get exactly what they expect.

Cancer—Pinot Noir

Those born under the sign of Cancer (the crab) are emotional, sensitive, easily hurt. Like their zodiac symbol, when threatened they will retreat into their shell. Cancers have a need to belong, and will go to great lengths to protect and maintain their home life. The temperamental Pinot Noir is known as the most sensitive varietal in the world of wine and when not receiving proper care will react adversely. If taken away from a home environment, Pinot Noir, like Cancers, will get very moody. Cancers are also known for being nurturers and extremely sentimental. So, Cancers, drink Pinot Noir: this wine will conjure thoughts of all things good and transport you to a place you'll never wish to leave.

Virgo—Sauvignon Blanc

Virgos are hard workers with neat, efficient and precise professional habits. They don't like to call attention to themselves, and while others may seek the limelight, Virgos are satisfied simply knowing their jobs were well done. Sauvignon Blanc is a clean, refreshing and straightforward workhorse of a grape variety. While never achieving the fame of Chardonnay, Sauvignon Blanc is highly enjoyable. And, like Virgos, don't fuss over it.

Libra—Riesling

The balancing scale is the sign for Libra. Librans require harmony in both relationships and their surroundings. They go to great lengths to avoid anything that might cause chaos. Riesling is like that—all of the elements must be in line for it to be great: acid, sugar and texture. Known somewhat as peacemakers of the Zodiac, Libras are charming and diplomatic and have a flair for bringing people together, whether it's for marriage, business or a dinner party. Riesling is similar, with its ability to pair easily with many different types of food. It is often "the peacemaker," bridging a wide array of cuisines from Sushi to Mexican.

Scorpio—Wines from the Nebbiolo grape

Scorpios are intensely emotional and live life to its most passionate, deepest and fullest. Scorpios can be suspicious of others, making it difficult for them sometimes to relate. This brooding, tough façade with passion just beneath the surface, is similar to the wines made with the Nebbiolo grape, Barolo and Barbaresco. The taste, especially when these wines are young, can be high in acid, tough and bitter. After aging, the wine becomes intoxicatingly fragrant with romantic aromas of roses and black truffles. All you need to do is be patient with wines of the Nebbiolo grape and with Scorpios because with time they will eventually unleash their sensual power.

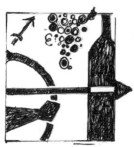

Sagittarius—Zinfandel

If you are a Sagittarius like me, Zinfandel is a wine after your own truth-seeking heart. The honest, independent and direct character of Sagittarians is well-suited to the robust, straightforward fruitiness and spiciness of a Zin. We Archers after all are not shy people, nor should our wine be! Wine experts believe the Zinfandel grape came to the U.S. from either Croatia or Southern Italy. This means Zin was also meant for travel-loving Sagittarians, who, with their optimism and jovial personality, are often the life of the party—just like a Zin with its rebelliously high level of alcohol. I don't have to tell you fellow Sags what happens when we have one glass too many, do I? Let's just say it's a good thing Zinfandel pairs well with the foot that often ends up in our mouth.

Leo—Cabernet Sauvignon

Leo "The Lion" is *King of the Jungle*. The only grape that can claim to be King of Wines is Cabernet Sauvignon. Wines made from the most regal of grapes are highly prized by collectors and critics for their rich full-bodied texture and generous fruit. Alas, with royalty can also come great ego, which Leos and Cabernet Sauvignons both amply project. A Leo boss is likely to take the entire office to an upscale restaurant for an extravagant no-holds- barred dinner. With caution thrown to the wind, Leos will order the most expensive Cabernet Sauvignon on the list. This act of generosity underscores Leos' taste for the finer things along with their preference for showmanship, pageantry and grandeur. Cabernet Sauvignon is a wine most definitely fit for a king, or, better yet, a queen!

Alpana's Journey

People are always very curious about how one goes about becoming a Master Sommelier. Well, I have to tell you that there is no official school you can attend or classes that you can take. You have to learn the job of becoming a sommelier from working on the floor in a restaurant, and not in a classroom. But before I talk about my own experience, I want to explain what a Master Sommelier is, and what it takes to become one.

The goal of the Court of Master Sommeliers was, through education, to improve standards of knowledge and service of potables in hotels and restaurants. The first successful examination for the title of Master Sommelier was held in the U.K. in 1969, and eight years later, by April, 1977, the Court of Master Sommeliers became known around the world as the principal authority for testing the qualifications of applicants. There are four tests which must be passed in order to achieve the top qualifications of Master Sommelier: they are the Introductory Course, the Certified Exam, the Advanced Course and finally the Master Sommelier Diploma Exam.

The last two levels—the Advanced Course and the Diploma Exam—involve passing three tests: service, theory and a blind tasting. In order to pass these two levels, the candidate is expected to speak with authority on the wine areas of the world and their products, to describe the various methods of distillation and the making of spirits and liqueurs. They're even required to know about cigars, to say nothing of demonstrating proper service technique, including decanting, food and wine pairing suggestions, salesmanship and tactful dealing with customer queries and complaints. The blind tasting requires identification, where appropriate, of grape varieties, country and district of origin, and vintages of six wines in twenty-five minutes. Depending on the level, the exams are given at varying locations around the country. The Master Sommelier Diploma Exam is held twice a year only, once in San Francisco and then in London.

It takes anywhere from four to ten years, or even more, to pass these exams. It took me six years. I want to emphasize that the exams are conducted by Master Sommeliers, which means the testing process is extremely nervewracking—not to mention how difficult it is: the final level has a pass rate of 3%.

I remember that going into one of my exams, I could not stop shaking and I thought my heart was going to pound out of my chest. Somehow I got through it and it was one of the most rewarding journeys of my life.

I can't express how great it is to set a goal and see it through to the end and accomplish it. But as with any goal, it's not the finish line that matters, but the journey getting there. So here's a brief account of my journey.

As I have explained, close to my twentieth birthday, I was hired as a wine clerk at Nielsen Brothers wine shop in Carmel, California. I worked there during the day and at Montrio, a restaurant, at night. Working at Nielsen Brothers offered me a great opportunity to become acquainted with the wine business. I would hang around and try to learn the lingo of the business when wine purveyors came in to show their wares. The store was pretty quiet during the day, so I spent most of my time dusting bottles when I wasn't studying. Since the wine in the store was arranged by regions, I played a game: I would clean a certain area, and then study it. It's much easier to learn about wine when you have the labels right there to look at.

Shortly after starting at Nielsen Brothers, I left Montrio to work as a server at Fandango Restaurant in Pacific Grove. Their wine list was much larger than Montrio's and included many more international selections. I had been at Montrio for three years, and I wanted to work in a French restaurant with more foreign wines. It was interesting working there, but it was also frustrating, because when I tried to recommend wines to my customers, they could not get past my age, and asked for Rene, the maitre'd who had a French accent, to help them with their wine selections. I was very discouraged, and when I learned that one of my co-workers was taking a month-long vacation in Europe, I decided to join her. I had never been to Europe. That month changed my life. I discovered what a joyous experience it was to have good food and wine as part of your everyday life.

When I came home from my month-long trek, I decided to stop waiting tables, and to go into wine work full time. As luck would have it, I had a friend who had taken a job at Rancho Cellars, a brand new wine shop in Carmel Valley, and who arranged for me to meet Jacques Melacs, the general manager. Jacques offered me a position as Wine Education Director, teaching wine classes and conducting wine seminars. The store was brand spanking new and the shelves were empty. For the next six months, we tasted anywhere from fifty to one hundred wines a day, tastings that greatly helped me to develop my palate: I was getting paid to study wine for a living! I remember reading up on a particular region at night and then having to go in the next day and teach it to my students. Talk about staying one step ahead! I loved teaching wine classes: it gave me insight into how people viewed wine and how intimidating the learning process can be. I found that if I kept the classes fun and hip, people tended to learn more and ask more questions.

A few months after starting at the wine shop, I went to take the exam for the Advanced Master Sommelier Course, and I passed it. Of course I was very excited to have passed the exam, but now I knew I had to face the real challenge of making it to the next, final level, the Master Sommelier Diploma Exam. One of the things the judges told me was that I would have to start working in a restaurant to improve my floor service skills—that meant I had to give up my comfortable job at the wine shop, and plunge back into the tumultuous restaurant world. I was only twenty-one years old, and I knew that even though I had passed the Advanced Course exam, it would be difficult to convince anyone to give me a shot at running a wine program, but I set out on a mission to try to land a restaurant gig.

For two years, I tried unsuccessfully to do this, going on interview after interview. The responses were all the same: I did not have enough experience, and I was way too young. I had just about given up hope of ever landing a full-time sommelier position, when I met Chef Jean Joho in 2000 in Carmel at an annual wine and food summit called the Masters of Food and Wine. This event featured some of the greatest culinary talents in the world and paired their dishes with some of the finest wines. Sommeliers from across the country were invited to work this summit, and I was one of the lucky ones. Every evening there was a party where everyone would just mingle, and that was where I meet Chef Joho. We chatted, and when he asked me what I did, I told him I was trying to find a full-time sommelier position. He gave me his card and told me to call him on Monday morning.

I called him on Monday, and that Friday I was in Chicago visiting Everest, his world-famous restaurant. He officially offered me the position of sommelier, and one month after that memorable meeting I had moved to Chicago. I had never been to Chicago, and I had never lived away from home, but I knew this was the opportunity of a lifetime and I had to take it. So I moved to Chicago with my blind faith, four boxes of wine books and two boxes of clothes—and that was it! At first I was really intimidated by working in such an upscale restaurant where I had to deal with prominent, influential people, but I realized that if I did my homework and projected confidence, the rest would follow.

I have to emphasize that I had never lived away from home, so I had to learn many things in my personal life, apart from my job. I had to adjust to things like paying rent and living alone without the comfort and support of family and friends nearby. Slowly I started to make friends, to get comfortable living by myself and handling grocery shopping, for instance, which I had never had to do.

The following year, I made my first attempt at the Master Sommelier Diploma Exam, and passed the service portion. The next year I passed the blind tasting test, and, in March of 2003, I passed the final part, the theory portion. I was now a full-fledged Master Sommelier. My hard work and sacrifice had finally paid off! That same year I was invited by the producer David Manilow, to audition for the role of host of the popular local PBS restauran show *Check Please!* I landed that delightful job and in 2005 I left Everest, but I wanted to stay with the Lettuce Entertain You restaurant group. So the principals, Rich Melman and Kevin Brown, created the position for me of Director of Wine and Spirits. Since the group owns and operates fifty-five restaurants, this is a job that carries a lot of responsibility and is a great challenge. But it also involves a lot of wine, and I couldn't be happier!